JIM LEE

DUNSTER
A castle at war

JOURNEY THROUGH 900 YEARS OF
AVAGE AND COLOURFUL HISTORY

JIM LEE

DUNSTER
A castle at war

A JOURNEY THROUGH 900 YEARS OF
SAVAGE AND COLOURFUL HISTORY

MEREO
Cirencester

Mereo Books

1A The Wool Market Dyer Street Cirencester Gloucestershire GL7 2PR
An imprint of Memoirs Publishing www.mereobooks.com

DUNSTER - A castle at war: 978-1-86151-142-3

Printed and bound in Great Britain by
Marston Book Services Limited, Oxfordshire

The address for Memoirs Publishing Group Limited can be found at
www.memoirspublishing.com

Cover design - Ray Lipscombe

The Memoirs Publishing Group Ltd Reg. No. 7834348

The Memoirs Publishing Group supports both The Forest Stewardship Council® (FSC®) and
the PEFC® leading international forest-certification organisations. Our books carrying both the
FSC label and the PEFC® and are printed on FSC®-certified paper. FSC® is the only
forest-certification scheme supported by the leading environmental organisations including
Greenpeace. Our paper procurement policy can be found at
www.memoirspublishing.com/environment

Typeset in 11/16pt Plantin
by Wiltshire Associates Publisher Services Ltd. Printed and bound in Great Britain by
Printondemand-Worldwide, Peterborough PE2 6XD

This book is dedicated to my mum, Peggy Lee, my children, Michelle and Martin Lee and Tomas and Melissa Lee-Eveleigh, and all the Lee-Hernon and Narayn-Lee family.

AUTHOR'S NOTE

Dunster Castle enters written English history in 1086 when William the Conquerors' great Domesday Survey mentions the castle. This is the first and, as far as the castle is concerned, the most important entry, telling of William de Mohun and his lands under the headline: 'XXV THE LAND OF WILLIAM DE MOION':

He himself (William de Mohun) holds Dunster and his castle is there. Aelfric (Anglo-Saxon thegn) held it at the time of Edward the Confessor and it paid geld for half a hide. There is land for one plough. There are two mills rendering ten shillings, and fifteen borders and five acres of meadow and thirty acres of pasture. It was formerly worth five shillings, now fifteen shillings.

The first two sentences are proudly inscribed on Dunster Castle's Inner Hall fireplace for all to see. It is interesting to note that there is no mention of King Harold, whom Duke William of Normandy had fought and defeated at Battle of Hastings twenty years earlier. William the Conqueror simply never recognised him as a king of England.

It was not until seventy-two years later, in 1138, with the struggles for the throne of England between King Stephen and Empress Matilda, that the castle itself first saw military action. Its near neighbours at Watchet and Porlock, however, had already suffered periodic attacks by Viking raids in the 10th century. It is from this time and the establishment of the Norse kingdom of York and Danish settlements in the east I thought it fitting to start the story, not at Dunster Castle but at Daws Castle in Watchet, which was built during the reign of Alfred the Great, King of all Anglo-Saxons, in about 871 and enlarged and strengthened at the time of marauding Viking raids on many sea ports of the Severn Seas in the 10th century.

CONTENTS

Preface

Introduction

PREFACE

The history of Dunster Castle and its nine hundred years of intermittent warfare is a fascinating account of the medieval stronghold and its relationship with events in the rest of Britain. Considering its remoteness from central authority in London, it has always maintained a position of influence alongside many of the larger castles in the United Kingdom, chiefly through its strategic location.

From the golden age of chivalry to the present era, conflicts in this country and abroad have caused the lords of Dunster to take up arms for King, Queen and Parliament through the centuries. In several instances these conflicts have come unbidden direct to the castle gates, with death and destruction in their wake.

I have not presumed to write a definitive account of the wars involving Dunster Castle, nor dwell on the social or economic aspects; rather to concentrate solely on bringing together an account of who fought where, when, and more importantly, why.

I have also included in the chapters events and activities the families would have found newsworthy enough through association; several of these dramatic and tumultuous events have helped shaped the western world today. These include the Crusades, Magna Carta, England's famous pirates and explorers, the Spanish Armada, the American War of Independence, Crimea and the two Boer Wars, not to mention the two world wars and numerous battles since, namely the Falklands, the Gulf wars and Afghanistan today.

Again, through close association, there is a chapter on the murder of Thomas à Becket, in which three of the knights came from West Somerset. The murder is illustrated in gruesome detail in the Luttrell Psalter. I have also told how this medieval family, as the owners of Dunster Castle, found themselves living in the time and place of the famous Robin Hood legends.

Another aim was to bring together the castle's wars into one publication which would be easy to read and understand. It would be just as rewarding for me if the events described stimulated further interest and research, as this relatively distant castle has had its full share of participating in the conflicts of Britain's past.

Perched high on a rocky outcrop overlooking sea, pastureland, meadows and wild open moorland and rising from its curtain of woods above the Avill river, the castle presents a silhouette of formidable towers, battlements and gables against a northern sky, dark and threatening. It is just as spellbinding when seen from the high street of the village and straggling up the slope towards the castle's lowest entry. This spot makes a dramatic and martial foreground from which stand out the wooded ascent to the Great Gatehouse and the cluster of towers soaring high above the treetops.

With documented archives stretching back over a thousand years, the castle is one of the National Trust's most exciting properties. Dudley Dodd, in his 1985 illustrated guide to the property, puts it dramatically by saying that Dunster Castle's

'embattled and turreted skyline is a frontispiece to English military history evoking the age of siege warfare, cannon fire, dark deeds, bloodshed, treachery and turbulent loyalties'.

I have relied on sources such as the Anglo-Saxon Chronicles, Britain's own Bayeux Tapestry in the Museum of Reading and the Gesta Stephani to tell the story of the medieval wars involving the knights of Dunster. The History of Parliament House of Commons extracts proved an invaluable source of information. Maxwell Lyte's *History of Dunster* was also a heavily-used source, as were the many already available publications on the castle's, and indeed West Somerset's, rich history.

I have tried to be factual, fair, reasonable and without bias, but it is inevitable that some events and statements may contradict this, whilst others may have been mis-stated or misinterpreted, especially with regard to the harrowing events in Scotland. I apologise in advance for any such errors.

INTRODUCTION

With documented archives stretching back over a thousand years, Dunster Castle in Somerset is one of the National Trust's most exciting properties.

In the great survey of England 1086 which provided an account of the Kingdom's wealth, the Domesday Book, compiled by William the Conqueror, mentions Dunster Castle and its Mill amongst the landholdings for Somerset. The history of Dunster Castle's nine hundred years of intermittent warfare is the fascinating story of a medieval stronghold and its relationship with events in the rest of Britain. Considering its remoteness from central authority in London, it has always maintained a position of influence alongside many of the larger castles in the United Kingdom, chiefly through its strategic location.

Only two families have owned and occupied Dunster Castle from the Norman Conquest in 1066 to the 20th century. The de Mohun family, of French Norman origin, built the original stone castle and for three hundred years administered their estates in Normandy and England from Dunster. The family eventually sold the reversion of the castle in 1376 to the Luttrell family. Since 1404 this family and its descendants have built, rebuilt and defended the castle through some of the most turbulent periods in the history of the British Isles, finally passing the castle and some 30 acres of meadow and pastureland to the National Trust in 1976. This book is about these two families and their knights, some in shining armour, others less so, and how they endured siege warfare, cannon fire, bloodshed, treachery, broken loyalties and glories in England and in foreign lands.

From the golden age of chivalry to the present era, conflicts in this country and abroad have caused the lords of Dunster to take up arms for king, queen and Parliament throughout the centuries. In several instances, these conflicts have come unbidden direct to the castle gates, with death and destruction in their wake.

I have ended the book with a tribute to The Green Howard Regiment (now amalgamated), which was first raised at Dunster Castle on 19th November 1688 and continues to defend the interests of United Kingdom in wars across the globe to this day. Until the recent amalgamation with Yorkshire regiments, The Green Howards were the oldest active regiment in the United Kingdom.

There have been, and continue to be, many excellent books on Dunster Castle's rich history, so I hope the reader will not be too disappointed if he or she finds little that is new. However, I hope readers new to Dunster Castle who wish to know in more detail about its families at war that this book will serve as a suitable introduction.

Dunster Castle has dominated the pattern of landownership in the parish and beyond, and although the castle is no longer an administrative centre and the land belongs to the state, the estate is still of major importance in the area. For centuries its owners asserted right as lords or overlords over many West Somerset manors and as lords of Carhampton Hundred, over the seashore too. During the 18th and 19th centuries in particular, the Luttrells bought the property of other landowners and small freeholders to become the major landlords in Dunster and surrounding parishes.

The large barony or honor of Dunster was held by the Mohuns and Luttrells with Dunster manor. In 1086 William de Mohun held 56 Somerset estates, mostly west of the Quantocks, but including Brewham, North Cheriton and Nunney in east Somerset and his ancestral manors in Normandy. The Luttrell lineage stretches back in unbroken succession to the time of the Norman Conquest and the family archives are an exceptionally complete record of their births, marriages and achievements, both as landowners and in their loyal service to England, with twenty-one generations of Luttrells and their descendants having lived in the castle.

Perched high on a rocky outcrop overlooking sea, pastureland, meadows and wild open moorland and rising from its curtain of woods above the Avill river, the castle presents a silhouette of formidable towers, battlements and gables against a dark and threatening northern sky. It is just as spellbinding when seen not from the river and meadow below, but from the high street of the village and straggling up the slope towards the castle's lowest entry. This spot makes a dramatic and martial foreground from which stand out the wooded ascent to the Great Gatehouse and the cluster of towers soaring high above the tree tops.

Dunster Castle enters written English history in 1086, when William the Conquerors' great Domesday Survey mentions the stronghold. This is the first and, as far as the castle is concerned, the most important entry. It tells of William de Mohun and his lands:

Here are Entered the Holders of Lands in Somerset THE LAND OF WILLIAM DE MOION. He himself (William de Mohun) holds Dunster and his castle is there. Aelfric (Anglo-Saxon) held it at the time of Edward the Confessor and he paid geld for half a hide. There is land for one plough. There are two mills rendering ten shillings, and fifteen borders and five acres of meadow and thirty acres of pasture. It was formerly worth five shillings, now fifteen shillings.

The first two sentences are proudly inscribed on Dunster Castle's Inner Hall fireplace for all to see. It is interesting to note that there is no mention of King Harold, whom Duke William of Normandy had fought and defeated at the Battle of Hastings twenty years earlier. William the Conqueror simply never recognised him as a king of England.

It was not until seventy-two years later, in 1138, and the struggles for the throne of England between King Stephen and Empress Matilda, that the castle itself first saw military action. Its near neighbours at Watchet and Porlock, however, had already suffered periodic attacks by Vikings in the 10th century. It is from this time and the establishment of the Norse kingdom of York and Danish settlements in the east I thought it fitting to start the story, not at Dunster Castle but at Daws Castle in Watchet, which was built during the reign of Alfred the Great, King of all Anglo-Saxons, in about 871 and enlarged and strengthened at the time of marauding Viking raids on many sea ports of the Seven Seas in the 10th century.

The coming of the Vikings

In 787 three Danish ships landed at Dorset. A royal official went to meet them, assuming the strangers had come to trade. Instead they killed him and sailed away. We now know this was the prelude to a series of Viking attacks that were to plague England for several centuries.

In case anyone should consider that there was a peaceful period at Dunster Castle and surrounding area before the Norman Conquest, we have to travel only a very short distance to the east or west coastlines to find all the horrors of pillage, burning and slaying by the Danish sea pirates. Porlock, Carhampton and Watchet were the Anglo Saxon towns in Somerset that bore the brunt of the Viking raids. Somerset stood firmly behind the Kings of Wessex, who spent many years fending off these ferocious invaders. In AD 878, when Alfred the Great was king and in desperate straits following the latest Viking incursion, which was made in daunting strength, the Anglo-Saxon Chronicle recorded:

'At Easter, King Alfred, with a little company, built a fort at Athelney, and from the fort kept fighting the force, with the help of those of Somerset who were nearest. In the seventh week after Easter, he rose to Ecgybryht's Stone, east of Selwood. All those of Somerset came to meet him...'

During this time of guerrilla warfare, undertaken from the Somerset Levels, Alfred is said to have 'burnt the cakes' of a local peasant woman while contemplating his future fate. He got a hiding for his trouble from the unsuspecting housewife

Viking raids were usually against coastal villages as they very rarely marched inland. By attacking the coast, they could pillage and take the spoils of war with them to their ships for the long sail back home. Their small, fast ships removed the possibility of the defenders chasing them. Porlock is first recorded as 'Portloca' (enclosure by the harbour or locked port), when, in the 9th century the Anglo- Saxon Chronicle records two attacks on the town: in the entry for 918 by the Vikings, and in 1052, when Harold and his brother landed from Ireland with nine ships, then sacked and set fire to the town, carrying off all that they could. Many people were slain, as well as thirty Saxon thegns.

During the Anglo-Saxon era Watchet became important enough to have its own mint. As the Vikings forced inroads into Wessex, many towns provided greater security by constructing fortifications known as burghs under the rules of Alfred and his sons.

Watchet became one of the ten important burghs of Wessex, as it is listed in the Burghal Hideage, a document dated c. AD 919: '…and to Watchet belong 5 hundred hides and 13 hides. For the maintenance and defence an acre's breadth of 16 hides are required. If every hide is represented by 1 man, then every pole of wall can be manned by 4 men…'

Even before the Danes turned their attention to Watchet, we have statements from the Anglo Saxon Chronicles (Winchester Manuscript) telling of a particularly fierce attack on the small hamlet of Carhampton, well within walking distance of Dunster village. Carhampton may have been the centre for a Saxon royal estate used for visits, with a royal court being held to collect local estate taxes. The Anglo-Saxon Chronicles refer to a bloody battle at Carhampton involving Danes with crews from 35 ships:

AD 836 Here King Egbert fought against 35 ship-loads at Carhampton; and great slaughter was made there, and the Danish had possession of the place of slaughter. And Hereferth and Wigthegn, two bishops, passed away; and Dudda and Osmod, two ealdormen, passed away.

The Saxon Royal Vill then moved to the next parish at Dunster before moving to Watchet. The old medieval track from Carhampton in the Dunster direction went over the hill to Gallox Ford and Park Street. The existing A39 road would have been under salt marshland. Assuming the Saxons moved the centre of administration from Carhampton to Dunster following these Viking attacks, the road pattern leads from Gallox Bridge and Castle out to the quayside (in Old Deer Park). The original road west to Minehead would have been St George's Street, a continuation from West Street, and before then Gallox Bridge and Carhampton track.

The Vikings sailed in longships with central masts and thirty oarsmen, fifteen either side. Sleek and fast, they were all-weather vessels. The longship gave the Vikings the ability to strike fast and be long gone before any response could be made by the local defence force. Long and slim, it could be rowed at about eight knots and, from around the 8th century on, sailed at about 20 knots. The shallow draft gave the Vikings the opportunity to penetrate deep inland, up rivers where previously the population had thought that they were safe from pirate attacks. These Norse pirates were disciplined fighters, but in their raids they slaughtered, burned, robbed and raped. They carried off the most beautiful women and took men to sell as slaves. Only the Kingdom of Wessex held out against them under the leadership of Alfred the Great, until the Danish territory called the Danelaw was established north-east of the frontier with Wessex and English Mercia.

From a vantage point on Dunster Castle's Keep Garden, the whole scenario opens with the Viking islands of Steep Holm and Flat Holm clearly visible and Carhampton and Watchet areas easy to identify, with the South Wales coastline prominent to the north.

The Vikings called the Bristol Channel the Long Fjord and gave the island of Lundy its name (Puffin Island). Viking place names are everywhere along the Severn coastline. Some places, among them Anglesey, Bardsey, Milford and Fishguard, were given Scandinavian names, and Swansea is said to have been founded by Sweyne Forkbeard, who was shipwrecked in the bay there. Forkbeard was the son of King Harold Bluetooth and father of Canute, the great Danish King and king of all England, famous for trying to hold back the tide because as King of England he thought he was entitled to sit on the sea without getting wet. Names of Norse origin can be found in the Gower Peninsula, including Worms Head - worm was the Norse word for dragon, and the Vikings believed the island was a sleeping dragon. Skomer, Gateholm and Skokholm islands on the Pembrokeshire coast also reflect Viking incursions.

Tusker Rock, an island in the Bristol Channel just off the coast at Ogmore-by-Sea, took its name from Tuska, a Danish Viking who inhabited the fertile Vale of Glamorgan with his fellow warriors. The names of Skokholm (Norse for 'wooded island'), Ramsey, Grassholm and Skomer islands also betray Viking origins.

The establishment of the Saxon mint at Watchet drew the unwelcome attention of these Vikings, who staged several raids between AD 918 and AD 997. During the 9th century the sea-cliff hill fort known as Daws Castle (now a Scheduled Ancient Monument) was built as part of defensive measures against these attacks. The remains of the enclosure can still be seen. They would have been more extensive, but much has been lost in landslips over the centuries.

The coins struck within its walls were part of King Alfred the Great's royal Saxon mints in Wessex, one of several in the region with Axbridge, Bath, Bruton, Taunton and Crewkerne among others. The first Saxon king to issue coinage from Watchet, the silver penny, was Thelred 11 (Aethelred), King Alfred the Great's father. King Alfred, born in Wantage, Oxfordshire in 849, was King of Wessex from 871 to 899. He was the only English King to be given status of 'The Great'. Seven years after he became king we read that in May 878 Alfred rode to 'Egbert's Stone' east of Selwood, where he was met by 'all the people of Somerset and of Wiltshire and of that part of Hampshire which is on this side of the sea and they rejoiced to see him' (Anglo–Saxon Chronicle). Together they defeated an invading Danish army which occupied most of the Anglo-Saxon kingdom of Wessex.

In the mid-10th century, the reign of Harald Bluetooth as King of a newly unified and powerful Denmark marked the beginning of a second Viking age. Large-scale raids, often organised by the Viking royal leaders, hit the coasts of England once more when the line of kings descended from Alfred the Great was faltering.

A fresh wave of Scandinavian attacks from the late 10th century ended with the conquest of this united kingdom by Sweyn Forkbeard in 1013 and again by his son Cnut in 1016, turning it into the centre of a short-lived North

Sea empire that also included Denmark and Norway. However the native royal dynasty was restored with the accession of Edward the Confessor in 1042.

Writing of several other Viking raids and great naval armaments the Anglo–Saxon Chronicles gives the following information:

[917]. Here in this year a great raiding ship-army came over here from the south from Brittany. And the king had arranged that there should be positions on the southern side of the Severn mouth from Cornwall in the south west and eastwards as far as Avonmouth, so that they durst nowhere seek land on that side. However, they then stole up by night on two certain occasions: on the one occasion east of Watchet, and on another occasion at Porlock; then on each occasion they were hit, so that few came away, except only those who swam out to the ships. And then they settled out on the island at Flatholme until the time came that they were very short of food, and many men perished with hunger, because they could not reach any meat. Then they went from there to Dyfed and then out to Ireland, and this was in harvest-time.

A.D. 987. This year was the port of Watchet plundered.

A.D. 997. This year went the Danes about Devonshire into Severn-mouth, and equally plundered the people of Cornwall, North-Wales (50), and Devon. Then went they up at Watchet, and there much evil wrought in burning and manslaying. Afterwards they coasted back about Penwithstert on the south side, and, turning into the mouth of the Tamer, went up till they came to Liddyford, burning and slaying everything that they met.

In the end Somerset played an important part in

defeating the spread of the Danes in the 9th century. King Alfred established a series of forts and lookout posts linked by a military road, or Herepath, so his army could cover Viking movements at sea. The Herepath has a characteristic form which is familiar on the Quantocks: a regulation 20m wide track between avenues of trees growing from hedge-laying embankments. The Herepath ran from the ford on the River Parrett at Combwich, past Cannington hill fort to Over Stowey, where it climbed the Quantocks along the line of the current Stowey road to Crowcombe Park Gate. Then it went south along the ridge, to Triscombe Stone. One branch may have led past Lydeard Hill and Buncombe Hill back to Alfred's base at Athelney. The main branch descended the hills at Triscombe, then along the avenue to Red Post Cross and west to the Brendon Hills and Exmoor.

A peace treaty with the Danes was signed at Wedmore and the Danish king Guthrum the Old was baptised at Aller. Burhs (fortified places) had been set up by 919, such as Lyng. The Alfred Jewel, an object about 2.5 inches long, made of filigree gold, cloisonné-enamelled and with a rock crystal covering, was found in 1693 at Petherton Park, North Petherton. Believed to have been owned by Alfred the Great, it is thought to have been the handle for a pointer that would have fitted into the hole at its base and to have been used while reading a book.

However, by 1066 the Danes had finally settled peacefully in England. All was about to change, however, because the Anglo-Saxon king, Edward the Confessor, had no son, and when he died in January 1066 storm clouds gathered and William, Duke of Normandy, who had a legitimate claim to England's throne, was waiting to attack. William had never recognised King Harold as king as he was only Edward the Confessor's brother-in-law, whilst he made claim through his grandmother, Emma, who had married the Anglo-Saxon king, Aethelred the Unready. Soon the Saxon hill fort at Dunster would gave way to a Norman Castle.

CHAPTER TWO

The Norman Conquest

The Norman Conquest was a pivotal event in English history. It largely removed the native ruling class, replacing it with a foreign, French-speaking monarchy, aristocracy and clerical hierarchy. This in turn brought about a transformation of the English language and the culture of England in a new era often referred to as Norman England.

Old English was the language of the Anglo Saxons, but following the Norman Conquest, French would become the language of commerce and power and Latin the language of education. The swiftness with which William the Conqueror subdued England and redistributed the nation's wealth is legendary. He entrusted the conquest of the south-west of England to his half-brother Robert of Mortain. Expecting stiff resistance, Robert marched west into Somerset, supported by forces under Walter of Douai, who entered from the north; a third force, under the command of William de Mohun, whose descendants were to control Dunster Castle for three hundred years, landed by sea along the Somerset coast. William had been granted 68 manors in the region and by 1086 he had established a castle at Dunster; this would form both the caput, or principal honour, for his new lands, and help guard the coast against the threat of any fresh seaborne attack, as well as controlling the coastal road running from Somerset to Gloucestershire.

In the period before the Norman Conquest, Somerset came under the control of Godwin, Earl of Wessex, and his family. There seems to have been some Danish settlement at Thurloxton and Spaxton, judging from the place-names. After the Norman Conquest, the county was divided into 700 fiefs, and large areas were owned by the crown, with fortifications such as Dunster Castle used for control and defence.

By bringing England under the control of rulers originating in France, the Norman conquest linked the country more closely with continental Europe, lessened Scandinavian influence and set the stage for a rivalry with France that would continue intermittently for many centuries. It also had important consequences for the rest of the British Isles, paving the way for further Norman conquests in Wales and Ireland and the extensive penetration of the aristocracy of Scotland by Norman and other French-speaking families, with the accompanying spread of continental institutions and cultural influences.

Duke William and King Harold were familiar with each

other, as they had fought together in France and some sources, such as the Bayeux Tapestry, suggest that the English lord had sworn an oath to support the Norman duke's claim to Edward's throne while in his service. Deploying his army, Harold assumed a position along Senlac Ridge, astride the Hastings-London road. With the army in line along the top of the ridge, the Saxons formed a shield wall and waited for the Normans to arrive. Moving north from Bulverhythe, William's army appeared on the battlefield on the morning of Saturday October 14.

Arraying his army into three 'battles,' composed of infantry, archers, and crossbowmen, William moved to attack the Saxons. His initial plan called for his archers to weaken Harold's forces with arrows, then for infantry and cavalry assaults to break through the enemy line. This plan began to fail from the outset as the archers were unable to inflict damage because of the Saxons' high position on the ridge and the protection offered by the shield wall. As William's infantry advanced, it was pelted with spears and other projectiles, which inflicted heavy casualties.

Faltering, the infantry withdrew and the Norman cavalry moved in to attack. This too was beaten back, with the horses having difficulty climbing the steep ridge. As his attack was failing, William's left battle, composed primarily of Bretons, broke and fled back down the ridge. It was pursued by many of the English, who had left the safety of the shield wall to continue the killing. Seeing an advantage, William rallied his cavalry and cut down the counterattacking Saxons. As the day progressed, William continued his attacks, possibly feigning several retreats, as his men slowly wore down the Saxons.

Late in the day, William altered his tactics and ordered his archers to shoot at a higher angle so that their arrows fell on those behind the shield wall. This proved lethal for Harold's forces and his men began to fall. Legend states that he was hit in the eye with an arrow and killed, while others believe he was slain by the sword.

With the Saxons taking casualties, William ordered an assault, which finally broke through the shield wall. If Harold was not struck by an arrow, he must have died during this attack. With their line broken and their king dead, many of the Saxons fled, with only Harold's personal bodyguard fighting on until the end.

In the Battle of Hastings it is believed that William lost approximately 2,000 men, while the Saxons suffered around 4,000. Among the Saxon dead were Harold's brothers Gyrth and Leofwine. The contemporary Song of the Battle of Hastings argues that four Norman knights tore off Harold's limbs and disembowelled him. Whatever the true cause of his death, the English bravely fought on, but without proper leadership, their cause was lost. The Battle of Hastings was the longest and most brutal in English history, and William's invasion marks the last time Britain was conquered by an outside force.

It is fairly certain that within a day or two news of the outcome of the battle at Hastings would have reached Dunster hill fort and hamlet, probably through pigeon post, which in the Middle Ages was the fastest communication system. Medieval dovecotes, or pigeon breeding houses, are found all over Britain. Another possible way of getting the news to Aelfric's retainers at Dunster in 1066 would have been through a high-ranking person at the battle sending an envoy with a written or verbal message.

There are very few contemporary accounts of the actual Battle of Hastings. Almost all accounts were written at a later date with the exception of the following, which comes from the Anglo-Saxon Chronicles (Worcester Manuscript) dated 1066. The following passage refers to the Battle of Hastings. The Chronicles simply state: '*1066. Here passed away King Edward (the Confessor) and Earl Harold succeeded to the kingdom and held it 40 weeks and one day, and here came William and won England; and here in this year Christ Church burned, and here a comet appeared on 18 April.*'

The following passage from another entry written just after the battle informs us in more detail:

Then Count William came from Normandy to Pevensey on Michaelmas eve, and as soon as they were able to move on they built a castle at Hastings. King Harold was informed of this and he assembled a large army and came against him at the hoary apple tree. And William came against him riding a black stallion and caught him by surprise before his army was drawn up in battle array. But the king nevertheless fought hard against him, with the men who were willing to support him, and there were heavy casualties on both sides. Then King Harold was killed, and Earl Leofwine his brother, and Earl Grythe his brother, and many good men... and the French remained masters of the field...

Yet another chronicler, a Master Wace, Clerk of the Church, was commissioned by King Henry II in 1160 to write an account of the Normans and their conquest of England. I believe he probably had access to the Mohun Chronicles. Wace has this to say about William de Mohun:

Be it known that in the year of the grace of our Lord Jesus Christ one thousand and sixty six, on Saturday, the feast of St Calixtus, came William the Bastard, Duke of Normandy, cousin of the noble king St Edward (the Confessor), the son of Emma of England, and killed King Harold and took land away from him by the aid of the Normans and other men of other lands; among whom came with him Sir William de Moion the old, the noblest of all the host, this William de Moion had in his retinue in the host all the great lords after named, as it is written in the Book of the Conqueror.

In the Prologue to Mohun Chronicle, William de Mohun and family are spoken of in these terms:

How the noble family of the Mohuns came with William, Conqueror of England, and how many great lords William de Mohun the elder had in his retinue then: and then the line of descent of the Mohuns to this day.

Aelfric, Saxon thegn and lord of Dunster, could hardly have avoided the fighting at the Battle of Hastings either. In Anglo-Saxon society, a thegn was a nobleman who held his land directly from the king in return for military service in time of war.

As William the Conqueror only redistributed Saxon lands to those who were with him on the battlefield, we may safely say that William de Mohun, companion-in-arms to the Conqueror, was also in the thick of battle.

After Hastings, William still had to conquer England. He marched from Hastings, crossing the Thames at Wallingford and then on towards London. At Berkhamsted he received the surrender of the city. William took hostages to ensure that the surrender was kept. As the Norman soldiers could not understand the language of the Saxons and the Saxons could not understand the language of the Normans, it was difficult for them to communicate.

William wanted to be crowned King as soon as possible. His coronation took place on Christmas Day, 1066 at Westminster Abbey, which had been built by Edward the Confessor. Duke William of Normandy was now King of England. He assigned to William de Mohun vast estates in the West of England formed by the aggregation of lands that had belonged to various Anglo-Saxons who had been killed at Hastings; presumably Aelfric was one such man. William de Mohun was certainly favoured by the Conqueror and the geography of his lands were particularly beneficial to him, as his estates in Somerset, Devon and Dorset meant that it was almost a straight line due south to Poole and thence to the Cotentin Peninsula and on to St Lo and La Moyen, his ancestral home in Normandy.

Events at Hastings soon spilled over into the west country, namely to Devon and Somerset, as Harold's mother, Gytha, led revolts against William the Conqueror, especially at Exeter, where the Conqueror lay siege to the city and confiscated all her estates and those of other prominent Anglo-Saxons. Gytha pleaded unsuccessfully with him to return the slain body of her son. The Conqueror banished her and her retinue to the island of Flatholm, in view of Dunster Castle, and thence to a nunnery at St Omer in Normandy.

Gytha's sons returned to the west of England two years later in 1069, with a fleet of 60 ships. Their attempt to retake Exeter was foiled by the Norman garrison in their newly-built castle and strengthened city walls. Frustrated, the brothers raided coastal towns of Somerset and Cornwall, where the Celtic Cornishmen joined them in arms and open rebellion. They plundered and ravished the countryside to such an extent that even the Saxons lost patience with them and joined in with the local Norman garrisons to expel them. The lack of local opposition made the brothers incautious, and they were caught and defeated by a large Norman force. In the battle and subsequent encounters the brothers suffered heavy losses and only a remnant returned to Ireland, thus ending the Saxon rebellion in the west.

Following the Conquest the king took much of the manor land into the forest law to create his own royal hunting forest, which included Exmoor, the Brendon Hills and the Quantocks. Under forest law it was an offence for anyone to hunt within the forest boundaries other than the king himself. This included William de Mohun, although he did make payments to the king which enabled him to hunt fox, hare and fowl, cat and badger. The king also took all rights to grazing, mineral and timber on his land.

William the Conqueror died after he fell from his horse in a riding accident in 1087, one year after he had carried out his legendary Domesday Survey. His body was taken to Normandy and placed in his great church of St Stephen in Caen. Towards the end of his life he had grown very fat and when the attendants tried to force his body into the stone sarcophagus, it burst, filling the church with a foul smell.

William de Mohun I, the progenitor of the noble house which held Dunster for more than three centuries and flourished afterwards in Cornwall and Dorset, took his name from Moyon, near St Lo in Normandy, where the family had considerable possessions until its separation from the crown of England.

The castle built by William de Mohun on the isolated tor which gave its name to Dunster, became the head of an important honour, or barony, comprising forty knights' fees in the reign of Henry the First, and afterwards enlarged. The manors retained in demesne about the middle of the twelfth century were those of Dunster, Minehead, Cutcombe, Kilton and Carhampton in Somerset, and Ham in Dorset.

Reverting to Domesday, it is interesting to find that William de Mohun kept thirty-six brood mares at Cutcombe and twenty-two at Brewham on the eastern side of Shire. He was Sheriff of Somerset at the time of the Gheld Inquest of 1084 and at that of the great Domesday Survey of 1086. Indeed it is probable that he held office for a considerable period, and that he was sometimes known as 'William the Sheriff'.

William's son, William de Mohun II, succeeded to the manors of Dunster on his father's death. His story begins when he attended the king's Council of Northampton in 1131. King Henry's son had tragically died in the White Ship disaster when it set sail in the dark and struck a rock, drowning all on board. Henry wanted his daughter, Matilda, to succeed him and rule as Queen of England, so in 1131, he gathered his barons together at Northampton Castle and made them swear an oath of allegiance to her.

Henry had been left with two choices for his successor: his daughter Matilda or his nephew Stephen. William de Mohun, in the presence of his king, dutifully swore fealty to Empress Matilda. Henry died in 1135 and the barons, with the exception of William de Mohun and a few others, broke their oath and asked Stephen to be king. Eventually, in 1138, this led him to make a direct assault on Dunster Castle.

King Stephen and Empress Matilda

The first English civil war began as a succession dispute between the Empress Matilda, daughter of Henry I, and her cousin, Stephen of Blois. On Henry's death in 1135 Stephen seized the English throne and held it for a number of years before Matilda wrested it from him, although she was chased out of London before she could be crowned.

With the help of his brother, Henry, Bishop of Winchester, Stephen quickly gained the support of the Church, and only three weeks after the death of Henry I he was crowned King. However, Empress Matilda did not give up her claim to the throne and Dunster Castle was one of her main strongholds. Matilda also had the support of the Scots under King David I, who invaded England but was defeated at Northallerton, Yorkshire. Meanwhile those barons loyal to King Stephen began building a hundred new castles and increased the size of their military forces. This triggered a major regional rebellion across the south-west of England, especially when in 1138 Robert, one of the most powerful Anglo-Norman barons, controlling estates in Normandy as well as the Earldom of Gloucester, renounced his fealty to Stephen and declared his support for Matilda, followed by William de Mohun.

The ensuing conflict was in general a series of isolated sieges, because every great noble held castles scattered all over England. King Stephen displayed great prowess in the field, but he often rode headlong against the nearest foe with no real plan of campaign. However, he fully appreciated the vital importance of controlling castles and he had a good grasp of siegecraft. He ravaged the West Country to deprive garrisons of supplies and made bold forced marches, sometimes even in midwinter, to catch defenders off guard.

The armies of Stephen centred on bodies of mounted, armoured knights, supported by infantry and crossbowmen. These forces were either feudal levies, drawn up by nobles for a limited period of service during a campaign, or increasingly mercenaries, who were expensive but more flexible and often more skilled. It was just such a force, led by the King himself, that came to one of Empress Matilda's strongholds, Dunster Castle, and attack William de Mohun 11 and his garrison in 1138 at the outset of the war.

It was at this time that many barons raised their own

armies, fortified their castles and joined in the struggle purely for selfish reasons, often plundering their neighbours and supporting whichever side they thought was winning. William de Mohun's Dunster Castle was no exception. Many towns and villages in West Somerset suffered heavily, and there was much brutality.

William had been accused of treason, and in the Gesta Stephani (Deeds of Stephen) dated to the mid-12th century and attributed to Robert, Bishop of Bath, a passionate supporter of the King, William de Mohun is singled out for some fierce criticism from the start. He claims William was the most notorious and became as ferocious a brigand baron as any in the reign of Stephen. The King is reputed to have joined in the name calling, dubbing William de Mohun 'a most predatory and utterly unreliable villien'. Anglo-Saxon Chronicle states:

In the days of this King there was nothing but strife, evil, and robbery, for quickly the great men who were traitors rose against him. When the traitors saw that Stephen was a good-humoured, kindly, and easy-going man who inflicted no punishment, then they committed all manner of horrible crimes. And so it lasted for nineteen years while Stephen was King, till the land was all undone and darkened with such deeds, and men said openly that Christ and his angels slept.

It appears that King Stephen actually approached the castle from the old medieval Carhampton to Minehead road, his army coming upon the brow of May Hill opposite the South Terrace across the Polo Lawns. In describing the events of 1138 and why Dunster Castle was attacked, the

Gesta Stephani has this to say about William de Mohun and the siting of Dunster Castle:

At that time, William de Moiun, a man not only of the highest rank but also of illustrious lineage, raised a mighty revolt against the King, and, collecting some bands of horsemen and footmen at his fortress, which he had placed in a fair and impregnable position by the sea-shore, began to overrun all that part of England in warlike manner, sweeping it as with a whirlwind.

At all places and at all times, laying aside his loyalty, he set himself to work his cruel will, to subdue by violence not only his neighbours but others living afar off, to oppress with robbery and pillage, with fire and sword, any who resisted, and mercilessly to subject all wealthy persons whom he met to chains and tortures. By so doing, he changed a realm of peace and quiet, of joy and merriment, into a scene of strife and rebellion, weeping and lamentation.

When in course of time these doings were made known to the king, he gathered his adherents together in a mighty host and marched with all speed to put an end to William's savagery. But when he came to a halt before the entrance of the castle [Dunster] and saw the impregnable defences of the place, inaccessible on the one side where it was washed by the tide and very strongly fortified on the other by towers and walls, by a rampart (vallo) and outworks, he gave up all hope of carrying it by siege, and, taking wiser counsels, blockaded the castle in full view of the enemy, so that he might the better hold them in check and occupy the neighbouring country in security. He also gave orders to Henry de Tracy, a skilled soldier, oft approved in the hazards of war, that acting in his stead, because he was called away to other business, he should with all promptitude and diligence bestir himself against the enemy.

Henry therefore, in the King's absence, set forth from Barnstaple, a town belonging to him and enjoying privileges granted to him by the King, and made vigorous and determined attacks on his foes, so that he not only restrained their wonted sallies and their unbridled, marauding raids in the neighbourhood, but also captured a hundred and four horsemen in one cavalry encounter. At length, he so reduced and humbled William that he was able to abandon further hostilities against him and to leave the country more peaceful and free from such disturbance.

Though Dunster Castle may have been reduced, William de Mohun himself did not bow to subjection and he remained loyal as ever to his royal mistress, Empress Matilda of Flanders. She, in turn, put such a high value on his services that in June 1141 she raised him to the rank of earl. Under the name of Earl William de Mohun he was witness to a charter issued by her at Westminster at midsummer the same year.

King Stephen died in 1154, the last of the Norman kings, and Empress Matilda's son Henry of Anjou became king Henry II, thereby ushering in the age of the Plantagenets, that long line of quarrelsome kings that was to endure until 1485. William de Mohun was now restored to favour and Dunster Castle was spared as Henry Plantagenet, Matilda's son, set about ruthlessly destroying those castles which had opposed him and before that his mother, the Empress.

Murder in the Cathedral

'Will no one rid me of this turbulent priest?' These were the words famously spoken by King Henry II when he received the news at his Christmas court in 1170 at Bures in Normandy, France. Four knights attending the council soon gave the king his answer. On the 29 December 1170, the knights, wanting to carry out the kings' wishes, confronted and murdered Thomas à Becket in Canterbury Cathedral.

Thomas Becket or St Thomas of Canterbury, born in London, England, on December 21, 1118, was the Archbishop of Canterbury from 1162 until his murder in 1170 by King Henry II's knights. The king had ordered his death for refusing to give the monarchy power over the church. Becket's death made him a martyr to followers of the Catholic Church, and Pope Alexander canonized him in 1173.

Three of the four knights who murdered the Archbishop were from the West of England, two of them living a stone's throw from Dunster Castle. Reginald FitzUrse , Manor of Williton, Somerset, was leader of the assassins, and the others were Richard le Breton of Sampford Brett, Somerset, William de Tracy from Exeter, Devon and Hugh de Moreville, an Anglo-Norman knight from the north of England.

Becket's death remains one of the most infamous events associated with medieval England and this association, as already mentioned, extends westward into Somerset and Dunster Castle and also eastward to Geoffrey Luttrell in Lincolnshire and the Luttrell Psalter.

Born within earshot of Bow Bells, and venerated for centuries as the 'light of London', Thomas Becket was the most celebrated medieval Englishman. His brutal murder – that of an archbishop in his own cathedral – shook 12th-century Europe to its roots.

Four knights had demanded the absolution of certain bishops whom Thomas Becket had had excommunicated. Becket would not comply. They left for a while, but came back at Vesper time with a band of armed men. To their angry question, 'Where is the traitor?' Thomas boldly replied, 'Here I am, no traitor, but archbishop and priest of God.' They tried to drag him from the church, but were unable, and in the end they slew him where he stood. His faithful companion, Edward Grim, who bore his cross, was wounded in the struggle.

The murder was reported in minute detail; no fewer than five of Becket's companions in Canterbury cathedral on that fateful day, 29 December 1170, wrote eye-witness accounts, the best of which comes from Becket's biographer Edward Grim. Grim was a clerk from Cambridge who was visiting Canterbury Cathedral on Wednesday 29 December 1170 when Becket was murdered. He subsequently researched and published a book, *Vita S. Thomae* (Life of Thomas Becket), published in about 1180, which is today known chiefly for a short section in which he gives an eyewitness account of the events in the Cathedral. He himself attempted to protect Becket, and sustained a serious arm wound in the attack. While there are four other accounts of the events of that day, Grim was the only eyewitness to actually observe the killing itself. Little else is known of his life, before or after the murder. Here is his account:

'The wicked knight leapt suddenly upon him, cutting off the top of the crown which the unction of sacred chrism had dedicated to God. Next he received a second blow on the head, but still he stood firm and immovable. At the third blow he fell on his knees and elbows, offering himself a living sacrifice, and saying in a low voice, 'For the name of Jesus and the protection of the Church, I am ready to embrace death.' But the third knight inflicted a terrible wound as he lay prostrate. By this stroke, the crown of his head was separated from the head in such a way that the blood white with the brain, and the brain no less red from the blood, dyed the floor of the cathedral.

The same clerk who had entered with the knights placed his foot on the neck of the holy priest and precious martyr, and, horrible to relate, scattered the brains and blood about the pavements, crying to the others, 'Let us away, knights; this fellow will arise no more.'

Murder of Thomas a Becket: The Luttrell Psalter

The British Library in London which holds the Psalter has this to say:

Psalm 26, f. 51

Psalm 26 opens with a 4-line initial as it is liturgically the first of the psalms to be read on Monday. This page was probably decorated by two artists, one painting the border and grotesques, and the other the illuminated initial and the scene in the lower margin. The scene depicts the grisly decapitation and the martyrdom of the popular English saint, Archbishop Thomas Becket, who was murdered while kneeling at an altar in Canterbury Cathedral in 1170.

This can be found in pages 5 and 6 (Psalm 26) where the fascinating illustration in which one of the knights, Richard le Bret from Sampford Brett, is shown armed with a falchion, a sword with one curved edge. Another, Reginald de FitzUrse, the leader from Williton, is in the front of the group, cutting into Thomas a Becket's head with a gold sword.

So a sword's crushing blow, as depicted in the Psalter, extinguished the life of Thomas a Becket, Archbishop of

Canterbury, on a cold December evening as he struggled on the steps of his altar. Contemporary accounts and subsequent history have laid the blame for the murder at the feet of Becket's former close personal friend, King Henry II, who had succeeded Empress Matilda.

Once dead, Becket was hailed as a saint, and his shrine became one of the most celebrated pilgrimage sites of western Europe, and the destination of Geoffrey Chaucer's pilgrims in the *Canterbury Tales*.

Before he left to do penance in the Holy Land and go on Crusade, Reginald FitzUrse gave half his manor of Williton to his brother and half to the knights of St John. The title deeds were said to be held initially in the vaults of William de Mohun (d.1176) at Dunster Castle. Becket's murder, the result of their action, led to the disgraced knights and their families doing a number of penances, one of which was to build a chantry chapel in the centre of Watchet and the building of St Decuman's Church, also in Watchet, which Richard le Bret and Reginald FitzUrse then gave to Wells Cathedral. Their families went on to give other lands to atone for their relations' evil deed. The building of St Decuman's Church, Watchet, and the land where the Knight's Templar new school now exists was originally given to the Order of the Knights Templar by Reginald FitzUrse in penance for his murderous deed .

It was believed that all four knights died within three years of the date of their crime. One tradition is that the bodies of the knights were returned to Brean Down, along the coast near Weston-super-Mare, and buried there.

Another tradition says they are buried beneath three mounds which can be seen on Flat Holm.

It is also worth noting one or two direct connections with Dunster Castle. Annora Luttrell, daughter of Alexander Luttrell (East Quantoxhead and Hinkling in Nottinghamshire), married c1290 a certain Ralph FitzUrse, her neighbour from Williton and direct descendant of Reginald FitzUrse.

In 1346, other descendants of the knights Reginald de FitzUrse and Richard le Breton, two of the more local aristocratic assassins, witnessed a Royal Licence along with Alexander Luttrell John Osberne, Constable of Dunster, to return former lands of Sir John de Mohun V back to him. Along with this gathering were William of Fordingham, the domestic chaplain of Dunster Castle, and Maud of Bourton, a personal attendant of Lady Joan de Mohun, who later sold the castle to the Luttrells.

The Crusades, Magna Carta and Robin Hood

The Crusades were holy wars fought between Christians in Europe and Muslims in the Middle East between 1095 and 1291, and their effect resonates with us to this day. Although the main goal of the Crusades was to take control of Jerusalem from the Muslims, there were many reasons why European knights and others were willing to travel and fight a war in a foreign land.

For centuries, Christian pilgrims travelled from Europe to Jerusalem. In the 11th century, however, the Seljuk Turks, who were Muslim, began to attack these pilgrimages. In 1071, the Seljuk Turks fought against the Byzantine Empire at the Battle of Manzikert. The Byzantines, who were Christian, lost. The Byzantine emperor asked the Christians in Europe to help protect his empire from the Turks. In

1095, Pope Urban II called for a crusade against the Muslims to regain control of Jerusalem. To all Crusaders, he gave this promise: 'All who die by the way, whether by land or by sea, or in battle against the [Muslims], shall have immediate [forgiveness] of sins'.

Through brief notices we learn from medieval documents of the de Mohun and Luttrell families' involvement in the Holy Wars. The first time we hear of Dunster Castle knights on Crusade comes from the Bruton Cartulary, when William de Mohun IV arranging with the Augustinian Canons of that Priory that his anniversary should be kept year after year after he stated his intention of going on pilgrimage to Jerusalem. It is doubtful it was a 'pilgrimage' in the peaceful sense. A pilgrimage in the middle ages was not a vacation; it was, and still is, a transformational journey during which significant change takes place, especially in the fortitude in the person undertaking it. It is more than likely that William de Mohun was part of the actual Crusade. His death in 1193 in Jerusalem, Palestine, was during the time of the most famous of the Crusades, that known to schoolchildren throughout Britain; the Crusade of King Richard, fighting against Saladin in the Third Crusade with the largest crusader army ever assembled.

On William de Mohun's death, the Crown, under King Richard I (The Lionheart or Richard Coeur-de-Lion) took possession of the Honour of Dunster, as William's successor and heir was a minor at the time. Whenever the lord was a minor the king took control of the barony and castle.

Between 1195 and 1203 the king paid the janitor and watch of the castle was maintained by Royal Order. He also paid an annuity to Richard the clerk by gift of William de Mohun of 34 mounted men, two crossbowmen and their horses, repairs to the mill, the cultivation of the vineyards and the wages of servants and for repairs to Dunster Castle in 1195 and 1199-1200.

Reynold de Mohun 1, the son of William, died in 1213 and his widow Alice married another crusading knight, William Paynel of Bampton, Devon, who died in 1228 during the Sixth Crusade when Jerusalem was finally taken with King Henry III on the throne of England.

There had been political trouble at Dunster Castle before. Reynold de Mohun I died between the death of Richard the Lionheart and the coronation of his brother Prince John, who, incidentally, had the key support of the Luttrell family in his struggle for the throne. When King John was in France in January 1203, he gave orders to the grand seneschal or Chamberlain of Normandy, Hubert de Burgh, to deliver all the lands of Reynold de Mohun he held in that duchy. We learn that at the beginning of May Hubert de Burgh was commanded by the King to warn and induce Reynold de Mohun to accept from the King an exchange of his lands in England for his land at Caen and to notify the king immediately this was completed.

Robin Hood

Closely related to the events surrounding King Richard I

are the Robin Hood legends, with the Sheriff of Nottingham and 'bad' King John. This is where the Luttrell family enter English history. In the later part of the twelfth century Geoffrey Luttrell acquired small properties at Gamston and Bridgeford in Nottinghamshire, close to Sherwood Forest and Clumber Park, Nottinghamshire, now owned by the National Trust.

Royal Sherwood features a wide range of landscapes. It includes the historic heartlands of Sherwood Forest, the extensive parklands and estates of the Dukeries and the estate farmlands south of the hill settlement of Blyth. The area is rich in historic and cultural associations, including those of Lord Byron at Newstead Abbey, the Pilgrim Fathers and of course Robin Hood. The forest is a remnant of an older and much larger royal hunting forest, which derived its name from its status as the shire (or sher) wood of Nottinghamshire (in Domesday, the forest covered perhaps a quarter of Nottinghamshire, in woodland and heath subject to the forest laws) which in fact extended into several neighbouring counties (shires), bordered on the west by the River Erewash and the Forest of East Derbyshire.

During the absence of Richard the First in Palestine, this Geoffrey Luttrell was in open rebellion with John, Count of Mortain (Prince John), and was consequently deprived of his lands when Richard returned from the Holy Land. He was, however, reinstated after the accession of the Count to the throne of England as King John, and from 1204 to 1215 he seems to have been continuously employed in public business in one capacity or another. Many royal charters of the period were witnessed by him as a person in frequent personal attendance upon the King. For a time, he had authority to issue writs in the King's name with regard to wine. He afterwards became the navy paymaster of the King's ships. In 1204 and again in 1215 he was in Ireland with large administrative powers. In 1206, he was in Poitou and Gascony as one of the King's treasurers.

However, before Luttrell's commissions, England was not in good shape in the late 12th century. King Richard I was being held for ransom by Leopold V, Duke of Austria. In his absence, Richard's younger brother Prince John had allied with Philip II, King of France. Prince John was trying to keep Richard I out of England for as long as he could. John wanted to build up his support in the kingdom so that he could eventually steal the throne from his brother, and did not even bother to keep the peace or hold proper trials. England was full of people recently returned from the Crusades, who had become used to violence and theft. This lawlessness was a real problem.

The Knights Templar and Hospitallers, with many of England's illustrious knights, were siding with Prince John. Because Richard's crusade had been unsuccessful in winning back Jerusalem from Saladin, the famous Muslim leader, these knights had abandoned him in favour of his younger brother. As we have seen previously, Geoffrey Luttrell was no exception. This lawlessness is embodied in the Robin Hood legends and the historical circumstances of the period.

In popular culture, Robin Hood, previously known as Robin of Loxley, along with Friar Tuck, Will Scarlet, Little John, Alan a Dale and Maid Marion, are typically seen as contemporaries and supporters of the late 12th-century Richard the Lionheart, Robin being driven to outlawry during the misrule of Richard's brother John while Richard was away at the Third Crusade. The Sheriff of Nottingham is another important figure both in legend and fact as it was his task to capture outlaws such as Robin Hood, either to ensure the safety of trade routes through Sherwood Forest or to keep them from poaching the King's deer. King John's sheriffs were tough men who were chosen for their powerful personalities, strong spirits and cruel behaviour. They excelled as military men and fighters and their task as his administrators and governors was to keep the populace in order and to raise taxes.

King John knew personally every one of the hundred or so sheriffs he appointed, some of whom were his intimate friends and most trusted advisors, and they were carefully chosen for the merciless job they did. The Sheriff of Nottingham was particularly disliked, and along with King John, his equally merciless master, they governed the midland and northern counties with an iron hand.

In some stories, the Sheriff of Nottingham is portrayed as having a deep desire for Robin Hood's lady, Maid Marian. He is widely considered to be the principal villain of the Robin Hood stories, appearing frequently alongside such enemies of Robin Hood as Sir Guy of Gisbourne. Few of these foreign sheriff interlopers were more hated than the clan of Gerard d'Athee, Sheriff of Nottinghamshire and Derbyshire between 1208-9, whose notorious distant cousin, Philip Marc, was his understudy. It was a position the two men seemed to relish. Philip Marc was castellan of Nottingham in 1209, having custody of Sherwood Forest and holding the office as Sheriff of Nottinghamshire and Derbyshire between 1209-1224.

In addition to raising money for the King's adventures abroad, the sheriffs were expected to clamp down on any hint of baronial rebellion, while King John was giving shires, castles and forest wardenships to his own people, much to the annoyance of established local families who had a long tradition of service to the crown. Royal Officers had always been feared, but these foreign newcomers were hated by the northern baronage with a passion, due partly to the fact they had been dispossessed of much of their lands. This meant not only the loss of lands - the revenue from them, added to the revenue on the property they still possessed, went not to them but into the coffers of King John. Adding insult to injury, many of the barons had paid 'scutage' in order to be exempted from these expeditions abroad. That mattered little to King John, who ordered that hostages be taken to ensure their participation.

Walter de Lacy had to give four hostages, who were entrusted to Engelard, while another hostage was William of Monmouth. In 1214-15 the barons were so dissatisfied with King John that they threatened war against him, which led to the Magna Carta of 1215, and another part in English history for Geoffrey Luttrell. Some scholars believe him to have had dubious loyalties at best and nefarious actions at worst.

Magna Carta

Magna Carta is considered the first document that guaranteed the rights of the average citizen against the rule of the King of England. It set the groundwork for English common law and, later, the US Constitution and the Bill of Rights, and is now embedded in all western democracies. The four surviving original copies are housed respectively in Dover Castle, Lincoln Castle, Salisbury Cathedral and the Houses of Parliament.

It was signed (royal seal) between the feudal barons and King John on a meadow at Runnymede near Windsor Castle. The document was a series of written promises between the king and his subjects that he, the king, would govern England and deal with its people according to the customs of feudal law. Magna Carta was an attempt by the barons to stop a king - in this case John - abusing his power and making the people of England suffer. However one source says Geoffrey de Luttrell is listed as 'one of the Barons in arms to procure the Great Charter of Liberties from King John A.D.1215'.

In 1215, John appointed Sir Geoffrey to be his sole agent in negotiations with regard to the dower of Queen Berengaria, commissioning him at the same time to join the Archbishops of Bordeaux and Dublin in denouncing to the Pope the rebellious baron who had recently extorted the Great Charter of English Liberties.

If it is true that Geoffrey Luttrell was one of those at Runnymede in support of Magna Charta (opposed to the King), would King John have subsequently sent him on the 'embassy to the Pope' (the Pope sided with King John and ex-communicated all of the Barons who forced the King to sign the Magna Charta)? Could Geoffrey Luttrell's death in France, while on this 'embassy to the Pope' be a result of his support for Magna Charta, in defiance of King John? That is, was he assassinated? However Sir Geoffrey was not one of the Barons who were sureties for the enforcement of Magna Carta, because under this clause, the Barons granted themselves the authority to overrule the will of the King and seize his castles and other possessions if necessary. His name does not appear on the list of the 25 surety barons at Runnymede. He is however listed number 37 of the other 200 or so baronial knights present on that day in June 1215.

In one of the documents connected with this business, Geoffrey Luttrell is styled 'nobilis vir', a noble man. His mission was so successful that Pope Innocent the Third annulled the Charter, suspended the Archbishop of Canterbury and excommunicated the barons, but it is uncertain whether Sir Geoffrey himself was one of those who conveyed the papal bull from Rome to England.

As a reward for personal services, Sir Geoffrey received from King John grants for life of the houses of a Jew, Isaac of York, at Oxford and Northampton, and those of another Jew named Bonnechose at the former. The King also granted to him some land at Croxton, in Leicestershire.

In consideration of twenty ounces of gold, he obtained property at Cratelach in Thomond, Ireland.

At some point, probably on June 19, King John put his seal on the final draft of what we call today 'Magna Carta' or 'The Great Charter'. In exchange, the rebellious barons renewed their oath of allegiance to King John, thus ending the immediate threat of civil war. Far from achieving peace, neither party seemed fully committed to abiding by the terms of Magna Carta. King John appealed to the Pope, Innocent III, who cancelled the charter in August 1215, declaring it 'as unlawful and unjust as it is base and shameful', so only a few weeks after it had been agreed, Magna Carta was a dead letter.

Armed conflict was renewed and the barons invited Louis, son of the French king, to give military support and claim the English throne. A year of civil war followed and was fought throughout England. At this point, the fate of Britain hung in the balance. If John had failed, not only would he have lost the Angevin Empire, but the kingdom of England would have fallen into French hands. It would have been the Norman Conquest all over again. But the King died of dysentery on 18th October 1216. With John out of the way, the regency council, led by William Marshal, declared John's son King Henry III. Geoffrey Luttrell, as we have seen, died the same year whilst returning from Rome.

In King John's time there was no parliament. Because the Magna Carta established the council of 25 barons whom the king was supposed to consult on matters that were important to the country, some people also believe it sowed the seed for parliamentary democracy in England. Even though John was not required to take the barons' advice, this did mark the beginning of power being shared by more people. The running of the state was now the concern of a group rather than an individual.

The Hundred Years' War with France

The medieval period encompasses one of the most exciting times in English history, and probably the most important event, after the Norman Conquest, was the Hundred Years' War in France. In 1337, Edward III of England started the war by refused to pay homage to Philip VI of France, leading the French king to claim confiscation of Edward's lands in Aquitaine. Significant battles included Crécy, the siege of Calais and Poitiers, as well as the victories of Henry V at Agincourt, while as usual, France and Scotland joined forces against England.

In Scotland, Robert the Bruce immediately ordered the destruction of Edinburgh Castle's defences to prevent its reoccupation by the English. Four months later, his army secured victory at the Battle of Bannockburn.

After Bruce's death in 1329, Edward III of England determined to renew the attempted subjugation of Scotland and supported the claim of Edward Balliol, son of the former King John Balliol, over that of Bruce's young son David II. Edward invaded in 1333, marking the start of the Second War of Scottish Independence, and the English forces reoccupied and refortified Edinburgh Castle in 1335, holding it until 1341. This looks like the attack in which Sir John de Mohun the V of Dunster Castle was involved in, as he did military service against the Scots in 1341.

This time, the Scottish assault was led by William Douglas, Lord of Liddesdale. Douglas's party disguised themselves as merchants from Leith bringing supplies to the garrison. Driving a cart into the entrance, they halted it there to prevent the gates closing. A larger force hidden nearby rushed to join them and the castle was retaken. The English garrison, numbering 100, were all killed.

When Edward III tried and failed to subdue the Scots he turned his attention to France. The experience of fighting in Scotland aroused mixed feelings in the men who made up the English armies. The cause in Scotland they saw as worthwhile and they were taught to think of the Scots as 'cursed caitiffs, full of treason'. Blood-curdling tales were put into circulation of atrocities committed by the Scots, generated a feeling of revulsion and hatred towards them. Also Scotland was considered an unattractive land; the weather was cold, the terrain difficult and the countryside sparse and poor. So it was with general approval that 1337 England switched the thrust of its attacks to France, beginning a long drawn out and intermittent conflict.

The Hundred Years' War was a series of conflicts waged from 1337 to 1453 between the Kingdom of England and the Kingdom of France for control of the French throne. Many allies of both sides were also drawn into the conflict. The war had its roots in a dynastic disagreement dating back to the time of William the Conqueror, who had become King of England in 1066 while retaining possession of the Duchy of Normandy in France. As the rulers of Normandy and other lands on the Continent, the English kings owed feudal homage to the king of France. In 1337, Edward III of England refused to pay homage to Philip VI of France, leading the French king to claim confiscation of Edward's lands in Aquitaine. Edward responded by declaring that he, not Philip, was the rightful king of France. After the defeat in Scotland John de Mohun V of Dunster Castle joined this new front and attended the English expedition into Brittany, in 1342, in the retinue of Lord Burghershe. Only a few years later he had the good fortune to be chosen, together with his brother-in-law, Sir Bartholomew Burghershe, 'the Son', as one of the founders of the Most Noble Order of the Garter.

We find him again employed, in 1346, in the retinue of the Prince of Wales, Edward, The Black Prince, when King Edward III landed in France. This is where the Black Prince and John de Mohun earned their spurs. At the battle of Crécy he was actually in the division of Edward,

Prince of Wales, which comprised 'all the flower of the chivalry of England'. One of his horses, named 'Grisel Gris', was a present to him for gallantry on the field of battle from Edward the Black Prince, eldest son of King Edward III. It is this horse that inspired the legend at Dunster Castle of Grisel Gris, the 'White Charger'.

The Battle of Crécy took place on 26 August 1346 near Crécy in northern France on the banks of the Somme, which in the 20th century became the scene of one of humanity's bloodiest conflicts. It was one of the most important battles of the Hundred Years' War because of the combination of new weapons and tactics used, especially in the pioneering use of cannon and the fact that the Battle of Crécy established the six-foot English yew bow as the dominant battlefield weapon of the time. It was at Crécy that cannons were first used in open battle, though some time before this rude artillery had been employed by the Spanish Moors in siege operations. The guns used at Crécy were very clumsy affairs, and were described by a French writer as engines which, with fire, merely threw little iron balls to frighten the horses.

The English knights knew the importance of being willing to fight dismounted elbow to elbow with the pikemen and archers, a procedure which was learned from the earlier Saxons and by their battles with the Scots, from whom they learned tactical flexibility and the adaptation to difficult terrain. The yeomanry of England there showed themselves superior to the chivalry of France, and the lesson which England had learned at Bannockburn she taught the world at Crécy. All of these factors made Edward III's army powerful, even when outnumbered by the French forces.

The English army numbered some 4,000 knights and men-at-arms, 7,000 Welsh and English archers and some 5,000 Welsh and Irish spearmen. The English army fielded five primitive cannons. Numbers in the French army are uncertain, but may have been as high as 80,000, including a force of some 6,000 Genoese crossbowmen.

The weapon of King Edward's archers was a six-foot yew bow discharging a feathered arrow a clothyard in length. Arrows were fired with a high trajectory, descending on the approaching foe at an angle. The rate of fire was up to one arrow every five seconds against the crossbow's rate of a shot every two minutes; the crossbow had to be reloaded by means of a winch. For close quarter fighting the archers used hammers or daggers to batter at an adversary's armour or penetrate between the plates. While a knight was largely protected from an arrow, unless it struck a joint in his armour, his horse was highly vulnerable, particularly in the head, neck or back.

Good tactical sense was another reason for Edward's success. He had taken care to avoid the mistakes his father had made that had cost him so dearly in Scotland at Bannockburn on the 24th June 1314. Instead of placing his archers behind the knights, who frequently got in the way, he placed them side by side, the knights usually in the centre, either mounted or dismounted, with the archers on their flanks.

The king himself took no active part in the battle, but watched the fight from an old windmill which overlooked the field. In the midst of the battle a messenger came in hot haste to the king, beseeching aid for the prince, who, he said, was hard pressed by the enemy. 'Do not send to me so long as my son lives; let the boy win his spurs; let the day be his,' was Edward's only reply to the entreaty. The young prince won both his spurs and the day.

When the battle commenced and the enemy advanced, the archers released a hail of arrows to break up the French cavalry. In the ensuing melée, John de Mohun and the other knights in his division moved in to finish the job. The defeat of France at Crécy marked the decline of the mounted knight in European warfare and the rise of England as a world power. From the river Somme King Edward I, followed closely by his son, the Black Prince, and Sir John de Mohun, marched with his army on to Calais, which surrendered to him in 1347.

The death of the blind King John of Bohemia, ally of the French, who fell with the chivalry of France on the fatal field, added another incident to the record of the memorable day. The veteran warrior, when he learned that the battle was going hard with the French, ordered his companions to fasten his horse's bridle to theirs and lead him into the thickest of the fight, where he and his faithful nobles fell dead together. The old king's crest and motto, which consisted of a triple ostrich plume with the legend 'Ich Dien' (I serve), were adopted by the Prince of Wales, and from that day to this have been worn by his successors.

These tactics were also used at Poitiers in 1356, by which time the English army had won for itself the reputation of being the most formidable fighting force of its day.

In 1348, Sir John de Mohun was again sent into France. By 1355, he was at Bordeaux, in the suite of the Black Prince. His name occurs frequently during that year in the household book, of which a fragment is preserved in the office of the Prince Charles, Duchy of Cornwall, and he is mentioned by Froissart amongst the witnesses to the King's letter, in 1370, for redressing wrongs committed by the army in Aquitaine.

Between the 14th April 1375 and the 4th April 1376 the robes of the Order of the Garter were directed to be issued to him. Sir Thomas Holland, afterwards second earl of Kent, was then in possession of his choir stall in St George's Chapel, Windsor. Soon after this, on 15th September 1375, Sir John de Mohun died. Edward the Black Prince died the following year. With Sir John de Mohun the senior male line of the family came to an end.

Sir John left three daughters. His second eldest, Philippa de Mohun, was a goddaughter of Queen Philippa of Hainault, wife of the king, Edward III. She had married three times; her third husband, Edward, 2nd Duke of York, had been slain on the field of Agincourt in 1415 as the Hundred Years' War continued to rage.

Edward was at the siege of Harfleur, where he made his will on 17 August 1415 before commanding the van on the army's march through northern France. He commanded the right wing at the Battle of Agincourt on 25 October 1415, during which he became the highest-ranking English casualty. His death has been variously attributed to a head wound and to being 'smouldered to death' by 'much heat and pressing'. Philippa de Mohun's husband was buried in the Church of St Mary and All Saints, Fotheringhay, where he had earlier established a college for a master and twelve chaplains. The monument now in the church was erected during the reign of Queen Elizabeth.

The Welsh Uprising

Civil conflict in England and the deposition of Richard II, whose father was Edward, the Black Prince, provides the background for the national Welsh uprising led by Owain Glyn Dwr (anglicised as Owen Glendower), who was briefly successful in liberating all of Wales from England. He was a supporter of Richard II, and the king's deposition and seizure of the throne by his son Henry IV angered Glendower, as Henry IV now declared his land forfeit.

The Glyndwr Rising or Welsh Revolt was an uprising of the Welsh between 1400 and 1415, led by Owen Glendower against England. He was defeated and English occupation of Wales was restored and maintained up to the modern era. It was the last major manifestation of a Welsh independence movement before the incorporation of Wales into England by King Henry VIII in the Laws in Wales Acts 1535–1542.

It must be borne in mind that Wales was only some fifteen miles away across the Severn from Dunster Castle as the crow flies, and as Sir Hugh's household accounts show for the year 1405, all his supplies and various proceedings in Somerset of his going into Wales to fight against Glendower were transported by ship. A brief timeline of Glendower's Welsh uprising and examples of Sir Hugh Luttrell's household accounts introduce us to Sir Hugh's involvement in these wars.

1400: The Glynd r Rising erupts in Powys Fadog, led by Owen Glendower, who proclaims himself Prince of Wales (16 Sep) and raids towns in north-east Wales (late Sep); after a few months of inactivity, the revolt spreads across Gwynedd.

1401: Conwy Castle is captured by Glendower's men. The Battle of Tuthill ends inconclusively during a siege of Caernarfon Castle.

1402: Battle of Bryn Glas; Glendower defeats the English, led by Marcher Lord Edmund Mortimer, who is captured and later allies with him. The English are driven from Wales.

1405: The English launch multiple attacks on Wales, retaking many captured castles. In August, Glendower leads a combined Franco-Welsh army into England, and reaches as far as Woodbury Hill before retreating.

1409: Harlech Castle, Glendower's last stronghold, falls to the English. Edmund Mortimer is killed. Glendower leads guerrilla raids across Wales and is never captured; he is believed to have died around 1415. Meredudd ap Owain Glyn D r accepted a royal pardon in 1421.

Sir Hugh Luttrell's father died shortly after 1378, and Sir Hugh's own career began a year or so later when, still a minor, he was retained by John of Gaunt as one of his esquires. He came of age in 1385 while abroad on royal business and subsequently transferred his service from Gaunt, firstly, by 1391, to Queen Anne of Bohemia, and then to Richard II. He received several grants of property from the queen because of 'her love for him', and no doubt he became a highly valued member of her household.

Glendower led a Welsh revolt against the English crown between 1400 and 1409 and was the last to claim the title of independent prince of Wales, proclaiming himself Prince of Wales in September 1400. He instigated a fierce and long-running, but ultimately unsuccessful, revolt against the English rule of Wales.

Sir Hugh Luttrell was an English nobleman and politician and an important military officer during the Hundred Years' War. He was a close associate of his cousin, Richard II of England, and was one of his most valuable advisors. He was also an esquire of John of Gaunt, and an extremely close friend to Queen Anne of Bohemia. Wherever he went provisions were dispatched from his estates.

It was also in 1402 that mention of the French and Bretons helping Glendower were first heard. The French were certainly hoping to use Wales as they had used Scotland, as a base from which to fight the English. French privateers began to attack English ships in the Irish Sea and provide weapons to the Welsh.

Rebellions in Wales, especially that of Glendower between 1400 and 1409, are testament to some Welshmen's continuing struggle for independence, although their own princes were replaced by English Princes of Wales from the time of Edward I.

In 1401, the revolt began to spread. The whole of northern and central Wales went over to Glendower. Multiple attacks were recorded on English towns, castles, and manors throughout the North. Even in the south in Brecon and Gwent reports began to come in of banditry and lawlessness by groups calling themselves the Plant Owain – the Children of Owain.

King Henry IV, on his way north to invade Scotland, turned his army around and by 26 September he was in Shrewsbury ready to invade Wales. In a lightning campaign, Henry led his army around North Wales. He was harassed constantly by bad weather and the attacks of Welsh guerrillas. By 15 October, he was back in Shrewsbury Castle with little to show for his efforts.

By the end of 1402 the rebellion was really heating up. 1403 marks the year when the revolt became truly national in Wales. Glendower struck out to the west and south, with village after village rising to join him. English manors and castles fell, their inhabitants surrendering. By the end of the year the French ships were raiding the coast of England, with Welsh troops on board, setting fire to Dartmouth and devastating the coasts of Devon. The Welsh and French had Dunster Castle in their sights next.

With Glendower in south Wales, Prince Henry, the future hero of Agincourt, burned his home in North Wales in retaliation for looting, pillaging and setting fire to towns on the West Coast of England. Rebel supporters were captured and executed during this campaign.

Sir Hugh Luttrell, like his de Mohun predecessors, found himself caught up in the war in Wales and also towards the end of the Hundred Years' War with France. In August 1405 he had been summoned to Wales, and victuals and six standards of his arms were sent there from Dunster the following month. He visited King Henry IV at Leicester, but was back in the Welsh Marches again at the beginning of October, only to ride home to Dunster Castle before the 23rd of that month. Three days later he went on a pilgrimage to a local shrine (Burgundy Chapel, North Hill, Minehead), presumably to give thanks for his safe return. The following year, on his second appearance in Parliament, he was made a member of a Commons committee nominated to treat with the King's Council over the terms on which merchants should be made responsible for keeping the seas, and shortly afterwards, in a related matter, he acted as an auditor for the discharge of the treasurers of war. In the same eventful Parliament he stood in as proxy for his blind cousin, the Earl of Devon. Wherever he went, provisions were dispatched from his estates.

Sir Hugh Luttrell's household accounts for that year supply various notices of his proceedings in Somerset and of his going to Wales to fight against Owen Glendower.

August 25: *'In the gift of my lord to a messenger of the King bringing to him his letters by which the King ordered him to hasten towards the parts of Wales, 3s. 4d. Also on the same day, paid by order of my lord for the expenses of the horses of the Earl of Pembroke returning from the King and those of other strangers, 3s. 5 1/2d.'*

September 11: *'In a cart twice carrying victuals from the castle to the haven towards my lord who was in Wales, 6d. Also on the same day paid for six standards of my lord's arms delivered to divers ships of Minhede carrying victuals to my lord in the parts of Wales, 2s. Also paid in the expenses of my lord and his household riding towards the King who was at Leicestre and absent for four whole weeks, £4. 15s. 8d.*

September 12: *'Paid to two armourers cleaning my lord's armour for fourteen days and a half, at 14d. a day, both of them and for a servant who waited on them (famulo eisdem servienti) for the same time, 16s. 11d.'*

October 2: *'In bread and ale bought for certain seamen who were in the ship (batella) Howell sent to the parts of Wales to get news of my lord who was there in the retinue of the King, 12d.'*

October 9: *'In 88 wheaton loaves bought and sent to my lord in the parts of Wales, every loaf at a halfpenny, 3s. 8d.'*

There followed several fierce attacks by Glendower supporters on English border towns, and a more general outbreak of rebellion in north-west Wales. The English were galvanised into action, and Henry IV arrived to lead a successful campaign against the rebels, although Glendower was never captured. Over the next few years punitive measures were enacted to keep control of Wales, but these were matched by many acts of Welsh rebellion - among them the capture of Conwy Castle in April 1401. In June 1402, at the Battle of Pilleth on Bryn Glas Hill, Glendower led his troops to victory over an English army led by Edmund Mortimer.

Disaster struck in 1408 when the castles of Aberystwyth and Harlech fell to the forces of the king, and Glendower's own family was taken prisoner. The Welsh nation that had existed for four years took once more to the woods with its prince once more an outlaw. Glendower, with his son Meredudd and a handful of his best captains, together with some Scots and Frenchmen, was at large throughout 1409, devastating wherever he went. No one knows what happened to him, but like Arthur, he could not die; he would come again. Henry V, the new king, twice offered the rebel leader a pardon, but the old man was apparently too proud to accept.

What is more remarkable than the civil war the revolt inevitably became is the passion, loyalty and vision which came to sustain it. Glendower's men put an end to payments to the lords and the crown; they could raise enough money to carry on from the parliaments they called, attended by delegates from all over Wales - the first and last Welsh parliaments in history. From ordinary people by the thousand came a loyalty through times often unspeakably harsh which enabled this old man to lead a divided people one-twelfth the size of the English against two kings and a dozen armies. Owen Glendower was one Welsh prince who was never betrayed by his own people, not even in the darkest days when many of them could have saved their skins by doing so.

Although initially very successful and rapidly gaining control of large areas of Wales, the uprising suffered from key weaknesses – particularly a lack of artillery, which made capturing defended fortresses difficult, and ships, which made their coastlands vulnerable – and was eventually overborne by the superior resources of the English. Glendower was driven from his last strongholds in 1409. There is no parallel in the history of the Welsh.

Continued conflict in France

Henry V became king in 1413 and in 1415, he successfully crushed a conspiracy by the Welsh to put Edmund Mortimer, Earl of March, on the throne. Shortly afterwards he sailed for France, which was to be the focus of his attentions for the rest of his reign. Henry was determined to regain the lands in France held by his ancestors and lay claim to the French throne. He captured the port of Harfleur and on 25 October 1415 he defeated the French at the Battle of Agincourt.

By the successive deaths of his grandmother, Dame Joan Luttrell, in 1378, and of his elder brother John soon afterwards, Hugh Luttrell became heir to the small paternal estate at Chilton in Devonshire, but he did not obtain actual possession of it until 1385, when he was in the King's service abroad. He was for a time an esquire in the household of John Gaunt, Duke of Lancaster, thus binding the Luttrell family evermore to the House of Lancaster. At the beginning of 1390, he is mentioned as a knight having influence at Court, and, two months later he took part in some jousts at St Inglevert near Calais.

The first year of Henry V's reign brought Sir Hugh Luttrell back into prominence, largely, it must be assumed, because of the impending renewal of war with France. His experience was of considerable value to the new King, though curiously, it was not until 1417 that he entered fully into his service. Before that time he had been placed in an awkward position. His appointment on the commissions of inquiry into the Lollardy political and religious movement in Hertfordshire, Somerset and Dorset must have put unwarranted strains on his personal relationships, in view of his close connections with several prominent figures in the movement. Indeed, the appointment may be seen as an astute step by the government, for as far as can be judged Luttrell, himself a religious man, was extremely orthodox. It is interesting to note that the King sent a special messenger to Sir Hugh to inform him of Oldcastle's escape from the Tower.

By 1402, he was acting as Lieutenant to the new Captain of Calais, the Earl of Somerset, and his receiver in Somerset sent 22 marks to him 'by the hands of John Luttrell, son of Richard, at his coming from Calec'. Later in the same year, Sir Hugh was appointed one of the ambassadors to negotiate with the Commissioners of the

French king and afterwards with the Commissioners of the Duke of Burgundy. Several of their letters have been preserved, and in one of them he is described as Lieutenant of Calais and, a short while later, as being appointed Mayor of Bordeaux. Luttrell remained Lieutenant at Calais at least until December 1403, when he was allowed to take quantities of green, black, russet and rayed cloth through the customs at London 'for his use and for the use of his household'. During the previous summer, however, he had spent some time in England, for his receiver had sent him 22 marks on his coming from Calais.

While still holding office as Lieutenant of Calais, Sir Hugh's talents were diverted to the field of diplomacy. He was appointed to at least four missions, the last of which is unusually well documented. In April and August 1403 he was commissioned to treat with the French over infringements of the truce, and in October, as a conservator of the truce, he was involved in discussion with his French counterpart over protection for fishermen. Two months later he was authorised to renew the treaty with Flanders. Six letters have survived connected with this assignment, comprising both complaints to the Flemish deputies and the magistrates of Bruges and reports to the King, the latter generally taking the gloomy view that the Flemings were not to be trusted. In April 1404, soon after the dispatch of the last letter, ambassadors from Bordeaux petitioned the Council for provisions and money.

Luttrell was regarded as a suitable person to organize

relief, and in the following month he was accordingly made Mayor of Bordeaux, with orders to depart for Aquitaine soon after midsummer. Accounts survive for the expenses of his voyage from Minehead to Bordeaux, but he cannot have been Mayor for long for he was back in England in October, being then elected to Parliament for the first time.

Through 1406–1414, little is known of Sit Hugh's activities. It is known that he was present at Glastonbury Abbey in 1408 with scores of other influential noblemen. It was then and there that Archbishop Thomas Arundel made a visit to them, and discussed important political and religious matters with the noblemen. In 1410, the Queen of England, Joan of Navarre, made Luttrell her steward, a task which he enjoyed.

Sir Hugh Luttrell's war in France was a continuation of the Hundred Years' War. When Henry V came to the throne in 1413, he gave a general pardon for his enemies in England and revived Edward III's old claim to the throne of France. The Dukes of Burgundy and Orleans were rivals for power in France and King Henry V allied himself with Burgundy. Prospect of another war in France did much to unite the warring factions in England.

Henry's military campaign in France began with the capture of the town of Harfleur at the mouth of the river Sienne. From there he set out with about 5,000 men, 4,000 of them archers, and marched to Calais. The English found their way barred by a French army more than three times as strong. Attempts to negotiate a clear road to Calais failed, so Henry resolved on battle.

Once again, against huge odds the English, longbow won the day. This was the famous battle of Agincourt, fought on October 25th 1415. The French had no order or discipline amongst them. Nobody would obey anyone, and when their own archers were in the way, the French horsemen began cutting them down as if they were the enemy. Some fought bravely, but to no avail, and by nightfall all the French were routed, with King Henry's banner waving in victory over the battlefield. It was over in three hours, with the loss of almost 10,000 French dead and 2,000 captured and only a few hundred English killed or wounded.

Sir Hugh's popularity increased in the meantime. He had travelled to France with the English army, to reincite the Hundred Years' War. He proved to be a daring leader, and was one of the key commanders at the Siege of Harfleur and at the Siege of Rouen. After the siege, he returned home to England, and in 1417 he entered the service of Henry V, becoming one of his most loyal retainers. Throughout the rest of his life, he would have a splendid relationship with the king.

The following entries occur in the accounts which used to be held at Dunster Castle but are now archived in Somerset Heritage Centre, Taunton:

1417: Paid to three Breton prisoners going into Britany for their ransoms and those of their fellows, for their expenses, 10s.

In the expenses of a French friar for six weeks, at 20d. a week, 10s. Also of six Bretons and a page, captives, of whom three for thirteen weeks at 10d. a week, and three for four weeks, and the page for ten weeks, 50s. 10d. Also of a man of Portugal for seven weeks, 8s. 2d. Of another from Portugal for two weeks, 2s. 4d.

For the expenses of my lord travelling to the sea, on the 8th of July, £7. 11s. 4d..

In the passage of my lord, paid for meat taken for my lord's hawk and expenses up to the same time, 16d. 27.

In the same year there is the following detailed account:

The barge called the Leonard of Dounstere.

The account of Philip Clopton, master of the barge of the noble lord, Sir Hugh Luttrell, knight, lord of Dounstere, as for a voyage made by her from the port of Mynhede to Bordeaux and back in the fifth year of the reign of King Henry the Fifth. The same answers for £42. 10s. received for the freight of the wine of divers merchants for the aforesaid voyage.

In paid for food, drink, planks, nails, wages of workmen, and other necessaries bought, and expenses, as in the repair of the said barge, in part by the survey of the reeve of Minhede, as appears by a shedule...£4. 10s. 10d. And in 6 pieces of 'tielde' bought for the covering of the ship, 13s. 4d. In 2 rolls of 'oleyn' bought for repairing the sail, 42s. In old anchors repaired, 6s. 8d. In 'canevas' bought for repairing the aforesaid sail, 7s. In empty pipes and 'barelles' bought for placing flour in, together with grease bought for rubbing the same barge, 11s. In 7 broad planks bought for 'alcassyng' of the same, 6s. 8d. In 5 oxen bought at 12s. apiece, deducting 5s. for hides sold, 55s. In 2 pipes of ale and other 'barelles' bought, 36s.

Other similar entries follow, the total gross cost for the voyage amounting to £42.3s.1d.

Fish were an important part of the medieval diet and a variety of fish including sprats, herrings, conger eels, rays and even the occasional sturgeon or porpoise were caught off Minehead Bay. When Sir Hugh Luttrell set again for war with France in 1419, the supplies sent down to his ship anchored off Dunster Hawn included thirteen and a half dozen ling and cod, one hundred conger eels and four casks of herrings. All this fish would have been salted to preserve it.

Two calls from the King for the supply of troops, the first in February and the other in April 1417, brought Luttrell into the centre of affairs.

In February and May his name occurred in council minutes as a 'miles constabularius' whose service might be required, and when the time came he embarked in the retinue of Thomas, Earl of Salisbury, with a following of his own numbering 20 men-at-arms and 60 archers. In the first indenture Sir Hugh Luttrell undertook, for a sum of £286 to serve the King in the French war for a year, with one knight, nineteen esquires, and sixty archers. The muster of his company, taken before embarkation a few months later, shows that he had serving under him Sir Geoffrey Luttrell of Irnham, the head of his family, John Luttrell, his own son, William Godwyn, his son-in-law, and sixteen other esquires, forty-two mounted archers and twenty-five archers on foot. None of the number were military tenants of the Honour of Dunster.

In June at Southampton, before they set sail, he had been appointed Lieutenant of Harfleur, which perhaps was then intended as the future base of English operations. There he remained throughout the ensuing period of conquest, and in the autumn of 1418 he received special instructions to enforce discipline in the garrison and hang all deserters.

In September that year he treated with the captains of Montivilliers and Fécamp for their surrender, and in January 1419 (after spending Christmas at home) he was empowered to receive the capitulation of the town of Montreuil and other places. Meanwhile he had been in charge of supervising the unloading of provisions at Harfleur and responsible for the appointment of a victualler for the town itself, and in March he was authorized to grant houses and vacant lands to such of the King's subjects as intended to live there. By July he had been promoted as Seneschal of Normandy, an appointment associated with changes not only in the financial administration of the duchy but also in the military sphere. As such he had powers (conferred in April 1420) to superintend the bailiffs, vicomtes, receivers and all other officers subject to Henry V in the region. Luttrell could grandly describe himself as 'Great Senescall of Normendie'.

He was still at Harfleur in June 1420 when he wrote to the King apologizing for not exercising his office 'as my will were' on account of illness, and congratulating him on his marriage to Katherine de Valois, an event which caused, he said, 'the gretest gladnesse and consolation that ever came unto my herte'. He went on to report on the state of the country, claiming that 'ther ys no steryng of none evyl doers' in the bailliage of Caux and the marches of Picardy. He mentioned that when the Duke of Bedford had landed in Normandy he had ridden to meet him and 'told hym the poverte of this countre', advising him as to the best ways of governing it.

Whether Luttrell's advice was well received is not clear, but it is notable that despite his important offices and long service he was not given a territorial stake in the duchy: indeed, only one insignificant grant, that of two houses in Harfleur, has been traced. He was replaced as Seneschal in January 1421 and probably ceased to act as Lieutenant of Harfleur at about the same time.

In 1421, he was relieved of his duties as Seneschal of Normandy and Lieutenant of Harfleur, and was ordered to return to England. Upon arriving in England, he met with many members of the English nobility and royal officials. There is at Dunster Castle an illustration by JHP Gibbs of Somerset Archaeological Society, 1981, depicting Sir Hugh Luttrell returning from the French wars with his complete retinue of knights and archers beneath his Great Gatehouse and 13th century Gateway which can still be seen to this day. He was also occupied with many royal assignments, which continued up to his death. In 1421 his kinsman, Hugh, Earl of Devon, permitted him to use his own heraldic arms, and Luttrell accordingly adopted the Courtenay crest and supporters. He was a trustee of the earl's estates, and after his kinsman's death he was appointed by the Crown as joint keeper of the warrens, chases and parks of the earldom during the heir's minority.

Sir Hugh Luttrell died on 24 March 1428 while on a visit to one of his daughters, a nun at Shaftesbury, Dorset. Spices worth 44s. were purchased at Shaftesbury, presumably to embalm his body, which was then carried to Dunster. The cortege passed through Bridgwater, where the churchwardens spent 12d. on torches. A further sum of nearly £10 went to the provision of white and black cloth to make gowns and capes for 16 poor people who attended the funeral. Luttrell's life was celebrated at Bruton, and a monument was erected to his memory in Dunster church.

Thus died one of the most outstanding West Country figures of the period and one of the most influential figures in medieval England. His career at Dunster Castle had spanned three reigns, in all of which he was prominent in different spheres.

The following account entries occur for the year he died:

Paid to John Bien of Shaftesbury by the hands of William Godewyn for spices bought of him for the burial of the said Hugh, 19 August, 44s. 1d.

To Thomas Wylhams for white cloth bought of him at the burial of the said Hugh, £6 4s. Also paid to John Slug for providing two oats against the burial of the said Hugh, 11s. Also paid to William Stone for white and black cloth bought of him, together with the making of sixteen gowns and the like number of capes for sixteen poor people at the time of the burial of the said Hugh, 74s.

A few months later, whilst Sir Hugh's wife, Catherine

and their six children were still grieving his death, the English army commenced the Siege of Orleans, prolonging the Hundred Years' War, but introducing arguably the most famous heroine in history, Joan of Arc. In May the following year the French under the command of Joan of Arc, now known as 'The Maid of Orléans', lifted the siege.

A skirmish on 23 May 1430, however, led to her capture, when her forces attempted to attack the Burgundians' camp at Margny. When she ordered a retreat into the nearby fortifications of Compiègne after the advance of an additional force of 6,000 Burgundians, she assumed the place of honour as the last to leave the field. Burgundians surrounded the rear guard, and she was unhorsed by an archer. She initially refused to surrender.

On May 23, 1430, she was captured at Compiègne by the Burgundians and was imprisoned at Beaurevoir, which is between Cambrai and St Quentin in the present day département of Aisne in the region of Picardy. The Burgundians, under John of Luxembourg, later sold her, for 10,000 Francs, to the English. Charles VII made absolutely no effort to rescue or ransom her. She was tried by the English for witchcraft and heresy and condemned to death by a tribunal of French clergy, headed by the bishop of Beauvais, who were sympathetic to the English.

Eyewitnesses described the scene of the execution by burning on 30 May 1431. Tied to a tall pillar at the Vieux-Marché in Rouen, she asked two of the clergy, Fr Martin Ladvenu and Fr Isambart de la Pierre, to hold a crucifix before her. An English soldier also constructed a small cross which she put in the front of her dress. After she died, the English raked back the coals to expose her charred body so that no one could claim she had escaped alive, then burned the body twice more to reduce it to ashes and prevent any collection of relics. They cast her remains into the Seine from the only bridge, called Mathilda. The executioner, Geoffroy Therage, later stated that he 'greatly feared to be damned'.

By 1453, however, the English had been almost completely driven out of France and King Henry VI had lost all his father's military conquests. The Hundred Years' War was over, but that quarrelsome royal family in England, the Plantagenets, soon had England embroiled in a bitter power struggle between the white rose of the House of York and the red rose of the House of Lancaster with, yet again, disastrous results for Dunster Castle.

A monument in memory of Sir Hugh Luttrell lies beneath an arched canopy carved in stone in St George's Church, Dunster. His grandson, Sir James Luttrell, an equally brave knight, was to be killed on the field of battle during the Wars of the Roses, yet still attainted for high treason, resulting in the loss of Dunster Castle and all its estates, the pride of his grandfather.

CHAPTER NINE

The Wars of the Roses

The name 'Wars of the Roses' is based on the badges used by the quarrelsome and warring factions between the two sides of the same Plantagenet dynasty, the red rose for the Lancastrians and the white rose for York. The Luttrell family of Dunster Castle were staunch supporters of the House of Lancaster.

In 2012 the skeleton of King Richard III, the last English king to fall and die in battle, was discovered beneath a Leicester car park which had been built over a long-demolished friary. He was killed at the Battle of Bosworth Field, Leicestershire, in 1485. Shakespeare had immortalised him in his 1594 play of the same name with the words he uttered on the battlefield, 'A horse! a horse! my kingdom for a horse!'

Around 1450, King Henry VI of England began to suffer recurring bouts of insanity. These proved increasingly crippling and led to the formation of a Council of Regency three years later. This was led by Richard, Duke of York, who was named Lord Protector and had a strong claim to the throne in his own right. Returning to sanity in late 1454, Henry resumed his throne and efforts commenced to reduce York's power. Believing Henry to be ill-advised, York and Richard Neville, Earl of Warwick, mustered a small army the following year and marched on London with the goal of removing the King's councillors. Striking Royalist forces at St Albans in May 1455, York won a victory and captured the king, who soon became mentally detached.

The breakdown of law and order under Henry VI was at least in part the consequences of the king's own personality. Effective government was nigh on impossible in the hands of a pious, weak king who, when he visited Bath in 1449, was embarrassed by the mixed nude bathing insisted upon by the enterprising local Somerset folk following the customs of ancient Rome. County rivalries fed on national politics. In 1451, the Earl of Devon, supporting the Duke of York's claim to power, left Taunton with a force of 5,000 men to attack the Lancastrian Earl of Wiltshire in east Somerset and then returned to lay siege to Taunton Castle defended by another Lancastrian, Lord Bonville, cousin of the Courtenay and Luttrell families. Lord Bonville surrendered to Richard, third Duke of York, who made claim to the throne. Richard was to be slain in 1460 at the Battle of Wakefield in an engagement with Sir James Luttrell's knights.

Sir James Luttrell's grandfather, Sir Hugh Luttrell, first lord of Dunster Castle, had done his training to become a knight at the age of 14 as a squire in the household of John Gaunt, Duke of Lancaster. This bound the family and its descendants to the House of Lancaster to this day and embroiled them in a disastrous conflict, the consequences of which they were to endure for almost thirty years. The treason of Sir James Luttrell and the tragedy of Lady Elizabeth Luttrell began soon after their fate was sealed when, in the Parliament that sat in November 1461, passed a sweeping ordinance against all the chief supporters of House of Lancaster. It singled out for criticism Sir James Luttrell, along with his companion-in-arms, for their part in the Battle of Wakefield. It stated that Sir James Luttrell 'With grete despite and cruell violence, horrible and unmanly tyrannye murdered the late Duke of York at Wakefield and to stand and be convicted and attainted of high treason, and forfeit to the King and his heires all the castles and maners and other lands of which they were or had been possessed'.

His grandfather, Sir Hugh Luttrell, first of the Luttrell knights of Dunster Castle, was a squire then esquire in the household of John Gaunt, Duke of Lancaster, and this has bound the family and its descendants to the House of Lancaster to this day. Sir James left Dunster Castle with his retinue and engaged Richard, Duke of York, at Sandal Magna near Wakefield on 10th December 1460.

Entrenched in his mighty fortification, Richard awaited the Lancastrians. York was aware that multiple Lancastrian forces were operating in the area. For reasons that are not clear, the Duke of York left the protection of Sandal Castle on December 30. Possible explanations for this action include a rescue attempt for a foraging party that was under attack, or a Lancastrian ruse which led York to believe that he had numerical superiority. In the latter case, it is thought that part of the Lancastrian army, led by the Duke of Somerset and Lord Clifford, advanced in the open across Wakefield Green, while the remainder hid in nearby woods.

Regardless of his motivation, York's forces emerged from the gate on the south side of the castle. Marching around the castle to deal with the visible Lancastrians who were approaching from the north, the Yorkists were soon attacked in the flank and rear. Quickly surrounded, they were overwhelmed and destroyed. In the fighting, York was unhorsed and killed, possibly by one of the knights in Luttrell's retinue who were closing in. Rutland attempted to escape over Wakefield Bridge but was cut down. The battle lost, Salisbury managed to depart the field, but was caught that night and executed in the Lancastrian camp. James Luttrell was afterwards knighted on the field of battle by the Duke of Somerset.

Precise casualties for the Battle of Wakefield are not known with certainty, but sources suggest that the Lancastrians lost around 200 men, while the Yorkists incurred 700 to 2,500 dead. In the wake of the battle, the heads of York, Salisbury and Rutland were placed on pikes overlooking the western gate of York. Though it was a decisive Lancastrian victory, Wakefield failed to end the dynastic conflict.

Seven weeks later, he again served under the victorious banner of Queen Margaret at the second battle of St Albans but was run through the stomach with a sword in hand-to-hand combat and died five days later. While casualties for the Second Battle of St Albans are not known with precision, it is estimated that the Lancastrians suffered around 2,000 losses while the Yorkists incurred around 4,000. Following the battle, Henry was recovered and his guards, which may have included Lord Bonville and Sir Thomas Kyriell, were captured. Having secured the king, Queen Margaret ordered the guards executed and had the young Edward of Westminster decide the method (beheading).

Fighting continued for another twenty-seven years, with the final actions coming at Bosworth Field and Stoke Field in 1485 and 1487.

The triumph of the House of York was disastrous for the Luttrell family. Henry VI was captured and locked in a dungeon in the Tower of London and died shortly afterwards, probably murdered. Within a week of his accession to the throne, Edward IV ordered the escheator who was charged with investigations into, and the management of, lands which had fallen into Crown hands in Somerset to seize all the possessions of the Dukes of Exeter and Somerset, the Earls of Devon and Sir James Luttrell. (Escheat is a common law doctrine which transfers the property of a person who dies without heirs to the crown or state.)

Later that year a commission was issued to Sir William Herbert to take possession of the lands of Sir James Luttrell, who was specifically described as a rebel. The Parliament which sat in November 1461 passed a sweeping ordinance against all the chief supporters of King Henry VI and named and once again singled out Sir James Luttrell.

In June 1463, King Edward IV, granted to the Earl of Pembroke, Sir William Herbert, a firm favourite of the king, the honour, castle and manor and borough of Minehead and Carhampton and the Hundreds of Carhampton and all other lands and profits to which Sir James Luttrell had been entitled in possession or reversion. It mattered not that Sir James was already dead, for treason carried a dual penalty: death and forfeiture of possessions. The grant was renewed and enlarged in March 1465, when some lands at Little Carhampton and Radlett were mentioned and the date was set back to 30th December 1460, as named in the retrospective attainder of Sir James Luttrell

Honours and offices of profit were showered upon the new Yorkist owners of Dunster Castle. In September 1466, a marriage was arranged at Windsor Castle between the Earl of Pembroke's eldest son William, who was only five years of age, and Mary Woodville, sister of Elizabeth, Queen of Edward IV. It was stated that the king not only dubbed the boy a knight but created him 'Lord of Dunster'. It is worth noting that William Herbert, the younger, is styled 'Lord of Dunster' in some royal letters patent issued during the lifetime of his father.

In July 1469, William Herbert, Earl of Pembroke and Lord of Dunster, was captured in a skirmish with Lancastrian soldiers at Edgcote in Oxfordshire. They then took him to Northampton and there beheaded him, along with his brother Richard Herbert. Lady Elizabeth, Sir James' widow, was left homeless with a young family to bring up, Alexander and Hugh, later Sir Hugh Luttrell. However she soon married again. Her new husband was Sir Humphrey Audley, cousin of Sir James Luttrell, and with the help of Duke of Clarence, the King's brother, she repossessed Dunster Castle, bequeathed to her by Sir James Luttrell.

In June 1463, King Edward IV granted to the Earl of Pembroke, Sir William Herbert, a firm favourite of the king, the honour, castle and manor and borough of Minehead and Carhampton and the Hundreds of Carhampton and all other lands and profits to which Sir James Luttrell had been entitled in possession or reversion.

After Sir James Luttrell's death, Lady Elizabeth Luttrell married his cousin, Sir Humphrey Audley, King's Esquire and Constable of Southampton Castle and brother of Lord Audley in Nether Stowey, Somerset. Sir Humphrey was taken prisoner at the battle of Tewkesbury and beheaded on the battlefield in a place still known today as Bloody Meadow. A brief summary of the battle follows.

On Saturday, 4 May 1471, the Lancastrian (red rose) forces commanded by Edmund Beaufort, 4th Duke of Somerset, supporting the intention of Queen Margaret, wife of Henry VI, to place her son, Edward, Prince of

Wales, on the throne, engaged the Yorkist (white rose) forces of King Edward IV at the confluence of the Avon and Severn rivers in what became known as the Battle of Tewkesbury. When the Lancastrian centre broke under the onslaught of King Edward's division, the Lancastrian army disintegrated.

It was every man for himself. Sir Humphrey Audley was among a small group of nobles who sought sanctuary in nearby Tewkesbury Abbey. Two days later, on Monday, 6 May, those within the abbey were removed and brought to trial before a military tribunal presided over by the Duke of Gloucester, as Constable of England, and the Duke of Norfolk, as Marshal of England. They were condemned to immediate execution as traitors and rebels. The sentence was carried out that same day and all were beheaded on a scaffold placed in the centre of the field on Bloody Meadow.

The Duke of Somerset, a personal friend of the late Sir James Luttrell, was the first to climb the scaffold, followed by John Langstrother, the Prior of the Order of St John, and then Sir Humphrey Audley. King Edward spared their bodies' dismemberment or setting up and licensed them for burial. Sir Humphrey was buried close to the altar of St James in Tewkesbury Abbey, in a space he shared with Thomas Courtenay, 16th Earl of Devon, who had died in the battle.

It is curious to note that Sir Humphrey's brother-in-law, John Courtenay, fought on the side of the Yorkists at

Tewkesbury and was rewarded for his services. Lady Elizabeth Luttrell was herself born into the Courtenay family and was a descendant of King Edward I through the de Bohun and Elizabeth Plantagenet families.

Even in those distracted times of civil war, there could not have been many widows who had, within eleven years, lost two husbands fighting on behalf of the unfortunate House of Lancaster, been evicted from her castle and made homeless with a young family to bring up. She eventually married a third husband, Thomas Malet of Enmore, on the Quantocks in Somerset, but according to common medieval custom, she retained the surname of Luttrell until her death in the reign of Henry the Seventh. She was buried before the high altar in Dunster Church. An incised stone slab, which has since been removed to the south aisle of the chancel, shows her attired in a sideless dress faced with ermine and a mantle lined with ermine, the neck bare and the head covered with a veil falling below the shoulders. Two angels support a pillow, and there is the usual dog at the feet. The inscription around it runs: "Pray, I beseech you, for the soul of Dame Elizabeth Lutterell, who died on the first day of the month of September in the year of our Lord 1493. Now, O Christ, we pray thee have mercy, and do not condemn the redeemed whom thou camest to redeem when lost".

Eight years before to Dame Elizabeth Luttrell's death, in August 1485, Henry Tudor, the would-be-King, sailed from France to Wales and gathered an army of 5,000 men. He was confronted by King Richard III and an army three times that number camped on Ambion Hill near Market Bosworth. The forces of Henry's stepfather, Lord Stanley, remained uncommitted to either side until late in the day.

Henry's forces attacked from the south-west and began to prevail. King Richard, in an effort to rally his troops and save the day, rode directly for Henry Tudor's standard 'to make an end either of war or life'. Almost face-to-face with Henry, King Richard was killed as Lord Stanley's forces entered the fray against him. After the battle, Henry was proclaimed King on Crown Hill at Stoke Golding.

Among the battles of English history, Bosworth is second only in importance to Hastings. Richard was the last Plantagenet king, and the last English king to be killed in battle. After Bosworth the Tudor dynasty reigned for more than a century.

Bosworth marked the end of the Wars of the Roses. There was no one else left to fight. It also marked the end of the feudal period of English history. With the death of Richard III the crown passed from the Plantagenet line to the new House of Tudor, Welsh in origin, and a new era of history began. Richard III was so loathed by his enemies that after his death at the Battle of Bosworth Field he was buried without ceremony and later his bones were thrown out and his coffin used as horse trough. Eventually his bones were interred in a friary in Leicester.

Kings were gaining the upper hand in the struggle with the barons. They encouraged the growth of towns and trade and took more advisors and officials from the new merchant middle class. This eroded the power of the land-based nobility. Further, kings established royal courts to replace local feudal courts and replaced feudal duties (which had been difficult to collect in any case) with direct taxation. They created national standing armies instead of relying on feudal obligations of service from vassals. Feudal kingdoms moved slowly towards becoming nations.

The next Luttrell to be involved in the aftermath of Bosworth was Sir Hugh, son of James Luttrell and his wife Elizabeth Courtney, daughter of Sir Philip Courtney of Powderham Castle in Devonshire.

The signal victory of the Lancastrian party on the field of Bosworth, in August 1485, revived the hopes of all those who had been ejected by the Yorkists. Henry the Seventh had not been on the throne many weeks before some of them were reinstated. Among them Hugh Luttrell, son and heir of Sir James Luttrell, presented a petition to the King in Parliament setting forth the claim that his father had been attainted 'for the true faith and allegiaunce which he owid unto the rught famous prince of moost blessed memory, then his soveraine lord, Henry late King of England the sixth,' and praying that the act of attainder should be repealed, and consequent letters patent made void. His petition was readily granted and the agents of the Earl of Huntingdon made way for the rightful lord of Dunster, in turn evicting the Yorkist Herbert family. To the Herberts the Dunster estate had been merely a source of revenue, and it is quite likely that they had allowed the older parts of the Castle to fall out of repair.

Hugh Luttrell of Dunster was created a Knight of the

Bath at the coronation of Elizabeth of York, wife of Henry the Seventh, in November 1487. A report on the ceremony states that the king 'made fortie & six Knights of the Bath. Knights of the Bath, to wit: three of his sonnes, the earle of Arundell, the earle of Warwike his sonne, the earle of Stafford, High Luttrell, and diverse others to the number of fortie and six'.

A few days later he received from his uncle Peter Courtenay, Bishop of Winchester, a grant of the office of Master of Poundsford Park, near Taunton, with an annuity of £10 for life. He was Sheriff of Somerset and Dorset for a year, beginning in November 1488.

Nine years later, he took the field against the pretender Perkin Warbeck under the Duke of Buckingham with an army including Hugh Luttrell which had been raised to repel Warbeck. Warbeck had landed at Whitesand Bay near Land's End, on the 7th of September 1497 with his wife and family and was joined by a crowd of the country people, who had been in recent revolt against Henry VII's excessive taxation. From Bodmin, with a small army gathering in strength, he marched to Exeter, but failed to force open the gates of the city. With his followers now 7,000 strong, he proclaimed himself King Richard IV. On hearing the news that Henry VII, the Duke of Buckingham and Luttrell's retinue were marching towards him he took fright and deserted his followers. With his wife and family he fled for refuge in the sanctuary of Beaulieu in Hampshire. It was here he surrendered.

His wife was kindly treated and placed in the household

of Henry's wife, Elizabeth of York. Warbeck was compelled to make two ignominious public confessions at Westminster, attended by Sir Hugh Luttrell, and at Cheapside in June 1498. On the 23rd October 1499, he was hanged at Tyburn after attempting to escape from the Tower with the imprisoned Earl Of Warwick.

It was in the Tower of London that King Richard, sixteen years earlier, had imprisoned his two nephews, known widely as the Princes in the Tower. The eldest, who was Edward V, was placed here along with his brother, 'for their own protection'. They were never seen again.

When Princess Catherine of Aragon came to England in 1501 in order to marry King Henry VIII's eldest son, Arthur, Prince of Wales, Sir Hugh Luttrell was one of the seven knights and gentlemen of Somerset who were selected to escort her from Crewkerne to Sherborne. At the subsequent royal wedding, also attended by her friend the Duke of Buckingham, who dazzled foreign observers by his sartorial splendour, Luttrell watched in awe as Buckingham strode around in a gown said to be worth £1,500. The next day Buckingham was nominated as chief challenger at an extravagant tournament .

In 1513, we find Sir Hugh Luttrell serving in the Royal Navy in the ship of Leonard Fiscaballi. At Minehead, Sir Hugh built a small pier and enlarged the harbour considerably, to the great benefit of the little town. In the reign of Henry the Seventh he was the Admiral there, and, on at least one occasion, he presided over a court of Admiralty for the decision of a maritime case.

War with Scotland

The Treaty of Greenwich, or 'The Rough Wooing', 1543–1551

This war in Scotland is one of the best-documented battles and skirmishes in the lives of the Luttrells of Dunster Castle and of the personal anguish and frustration John Luttrell faced as a commander. The war also saw the last pitched battle between these two sovereign nations before the Union of the Crowns in 1603, and begins with a treaty between the two independent countries.

The Treaty of Greenwich, also known as The Treaties of Greenwich, contained two agreements, both signed on 1st July 1543 at Greenwich Palace between the Lairds of Scotland and representatives of the English Parliament. This accord was a plan by Henry VIII to unite the Kingdoms of Scotland and England, that is, Union of the Crowns. This would have been, in effect, the annexation of Scotland by England.

The first sub-treaty helped to establish peace between these Kingdoms. The second sub-treaty was a marriage proposal between Edward VI of England and Mary Queen of Scots. In this part of the treaty, it was agreed that Mary would be accompanied at all times by an English nobleman and his wife until she was ten years old. Afterwards, Mary would travel to England and reside there until the time of her marriage. The Earl of Arran signed the accord on 1st July and ratified it on August 25th 1543, but the Scottish parliament ultimately rejected the treaty on 11th December 1543.

In May 1544, Henry VIII tried to avenge this rejection by a policy aptly termed 'the Rough Wooing', by which he planned a programme of devastation of Scottish territory. The orders given to his commanders make clear in no uncertain terms and strike a note of ruthlessness which chills the spirit, the English records indeed making it clear that their armies were remarkably successful in carrying out this 'scorched earth' policy.

So it was off to war in Scotland for Sir John Luttrell to do the king's bidding. John Luttrell was born in 1519 at Dunster, the eldest son of the family. John Luttrell must have emerged from his early career with an excellent reputation, for when the Duke of Somerset landed once more on Scottish soil in 1547 with an invasion force of professional soldiers he was made its Provost-General, a surprising appointment for one so young.

These were the instructions Henry VIII gave to the Earl of Hertford to carry out the 'Rough Wooing', written in 1544:

Put all to fire and sword! Steal everything you can from Edinburgh, then burn it and knock it down. This will always remind the Scots of their punishment for being disloyal. Do what you can to knock down the Castle and burn the Palace at Holyrood. Ruin as many villages around Edinburgh as you can. Destroy Leith! And burn and subvert it and all the rest, putting man, woman and child to fire and sword without exception. Then pass over to Fife and destroy all towns and villages the same way. Destroy St Andrews and spare nobody who is friendly or related to Cardinal Beaton.

Immediately after putting Edinburgh to fire and the sword, John Luttrell was knighted at Leith by the Earl of Hertford, King Henry VIII's lieutenant in Scotland. Thomas Wyndham, Sir John Luttrell's half-uncle, also distinguished himself by burning a convent and bringing away the nuns and the gentlemen's daughters who were at school there.

Sir John was with the army that assembled at Newcastle upon Tyne and Gateshead. In April 1544, Sir Christopher Morris reported to Lord Hertford that he had organised munitions for the invasion at Berwick upon Tweed. These included;

- 2 batard culverins
- 3 sakers
- 8 falcons
- a falconette
- 4 carriages with two 'bases' on each
- 3000 bows, 1000 ready strung in 60 chests

- 4000 sheaves of arrows in 80 chests
- 4 barrels of bow strings; described further as 40 gross of 12 dozen, ie 5,760 strings
- 480 Moorish pikes
- 3000 Bills.

Anthony Neville of South Leverton was appointed Surveyor General of Victuals for the army. Edward Shelley (who was one of first English soldiers to be killed at the Battle of Pinkie) reported that he had 40 thousand-weight of biscuit on 20 April.

At Berwick, Shelley had problems getting enough coal or wood for baking and brewing. He had to ask permission to impress more supplies and hold sales to rotate his stock. 4000 border horsemen waited at Berwick for Hertford's signal. At first it was planned that they would make a diversionary attack on Haddington.

Their commander, Ralph Eure, wrote from Alnwick on 28 April that these 'countrymen' were so poor he had to lend them money. He also asked for 1000 Yorkshire archers as reinforcement so that they could come to Edinburgh to support the landing. In the event, it was agreed that Hertford would summon Eure when he had disembarked his troops. When Eure's men arrived in Edinburgh they would get their pay.

On 10th September 1547 the Scots suffered a terrible defeat at the Battle of Pinkie Cleugh, the infamous massacre fought near Edinburgh. They came under fire from English longbowmen, artillery and naval bombardment from English ships anchored offshore, resulting in the infamous massacre of Pinkie Cleugh.

On the morning of Saturday 10 September, Somerset advanced his army to close up with the detachment at Inveresk. He found that Arran had moved his army across the Esk by the 'Roman bridge', and was advancing rapidly to meet him. Arran knew himself to be outmatched in artillery and therefore tried to force close combat before the English artillery could deploy.

Arran's left wing came under fire from English ships offshore (their advance meant that the guns on their former position could no longer protect them). They were thrown into disorder, and were pushed into Arran's own division in the centre.

On the other flank, Somerset threw in his cavalry to delay the Scots' advance. The Scottish pikemen drove them off and inflicted heavy casualties on the English horsemen. Lord Grey himself was wounded by a pike thrust through the throat and into his mouth.

However, the Scottish army was now stalled and under heavy fire on three sides from ships' cannon, artillery, arquebusiers and archers, to which they could not reply. When they broke, the English cavalry rejoined the battle, following a vanguard of 300 experienced soldiers under the command of Sir John Luttrell. Many of the retreating Scots were slaughtered or drowned as they tried to swim the fast-flowing Esk or cross the bogs. The English eye-witness William Patten described the slaughter inflicted on the Scots:

Soon after this notable strewing of footmen's weapons, began a pitiful sight of the dead corpses lying dispersed abroad, some their legs off, some but houghed, and left lying half-dead, some thrust quite through the body, others the arms cut off, diverse their necks half asunder, many their heads cloven, of sundry the brains pasht out, some others again their heads quite off, with other many kinds of killing.

After that and further in chase, all for the most part killed either in the head or in the neck, for our horsemen could not well reach the lower with their swords. And thus with blood and slaughter of the enemy, this chase was continued five miles in length westward from the place of their standing, which was in the fallow fields of Inveresk until Edinburgh Park and well nigh to the gates of the town itself and unto Leith, and in breadth nigh 4 miles, from the Firth sands up toward Dalkeith southward. In all which space, the dead bodies lay as thick as a man may note cattle grazing in a full replenished pasture.

The river ran all red with blood, so that in the same chase were counted, as well by some of our men that somewhat diligently did mark it as by some of them taken prisoners, that very much did lament it, to have been slain about 14 thousand. In all this compass of ground what with weapons, arms, hands, legs, heads, blood and dead bodies, their flight might have been easily tracked to every of their three refuges. And for the smallness of our number and the shortness of the time (which was scant five hours, from one to well nigh six) the mortality was so great, as it was thought, the like aforetime not to have been seen.

To all of Scotland it became known as Black Saturday, and it is remembered still to this day. The National Trust for Scotland hosts the Commemoration at Pinkie Cleugh Memorial Stone every year on September 10th. The National Trust for Scotland simply states:

The Battle of Pinkie was the final major battle fought between the separate Kingdom of Scotland and England before the Union of the Crowns in 1603. The battle was a dramatic defeat for the Scots with the virtual destruction of their 23,000 strong army. However, the English king Henry VIII still didn't achieve his aims of forcing a marriage between his son and Mary Queen of Scots, and Mary fled to France.

The young Mary Queen of Scots was quickly and secretly taken from Stirling Castle and sent to France. Parliament in London was informed that Sir John Luttrell 'took the Queen of Scotland prisoner on the field of battle'. Of course this simply wasn't true. This 'rough wooing' left in southern Scotland a hatred for the English which was to endure for centuries after they left Scotland in flames, their lands devastated and the tombs of their forefathers desecrated and destroyed.

A week after the Battle of Pinkie, Sir John was placed in command of the little island of Inchcolm in the estuary of the Forth, some two miles from Aberdour and six from Leith. The Augustinian canons, who inhabited it had evacuated it, removing apparently to Donisbristle. The canons regular of St Columba, Inchcolm enlisted the help of the great Abbey in Paisley dedicated to St Mirin to throw the English invaders out. Sir John Luttrell goes out of his way to pour forth his grievances to Protector Somerset having already complained of lack of biscuits, beer, butter, horses, carts, masons and money. In a letter written to Parliament on 30th April 1548 he states that the "Abbott of Pasle [Paisley] came hither with Frenchmen to scale the forte and brought with him all hys adherents off (sic) Fyfe, so that with the French and Scottys they were 2 thousand footmen and 500 horse". The Scots had intended to blockade the Forth so that when Sir John Luttrell ran out of supplies and ammunition they could make a direct assault on his positions.

The year before, in 1547, a contemporary Scots chronicler had chided Sir John Luttrell for substituting soldiers on the island for men of peace and of religion:

Sir John Luttrell, knight, having bene, by my Lordes grace and the counsell, elect abbot, by God's sufferance, of the monastery of Sainct Coomes Ins afore remembered, in the afternoon of this day (Saturday, 17th September) departed towards the island, to be stalled in his see thear accordingly; and had with him coovent of 100 hakbutters and 50 pioneers to kepe his house and land thear, and 2 rowe barkes well furnished with ammunicion, and 70 mariners for them to kepe his waters; whereby it is thought he shall soon becum a prelate of great power. The perfytness of his religion is not alwaies to tarry at home, but sumtime to rowe out abrode a visitacion, and, when he goithe, I have heard say, he taketh alweyes his sumners in barke with hym, which are very open mouthed and never talk but they are heard a mile of; so that either for loove of his blessynges or fear of his cursinges, he is like to be the souveraigne over most part of his neighbours.

In point of fact, the garrison established in the old

abbey of Inchcolm soon became a cause of anxiety to the English commanders. Instead of being able to control the navigation of the Western Forth, Sir John Luttrell was for a time invested by a leaguer of Scottish ships and boat, under an abbot and James Dogge, who were optimistic of capturing the rock. Although no assault was actually made, Sir John found himself almost powerless in the face of two men of war, one of them of 80 tons burden. He writes:

Having sent the Sacre to England, to procure timber, coal and other necessaries, I had only the Double Rose, which was 'lytell and open.'… 'Ther ys nothinge,' he writes on the 2nd of November, *'thatt grevys me so myche as that I cannott have on suyche shyppe, wythe my pynnays, as the Wyllyby ys…wyche yf I had had, the prisys that I have lost wold have paid ther chargys for 4 or 5 monythys.*

In another letter of the same date, he describes to the Protector Somerset his attempt to take a French ship 'of 2 toppys' that had failed to get into harbour at low tide. The pinnace from Inchcolm 'bett herr wyth herr artyllerye and shotte so often thoroghe and alongeshypp of the Frenche menne that they gave greate cryes wythynn borde and ranne herr ashore agaynst the chapyl att Lythe, where the pynnys bett herr still thorow wythyn poynte blancke, and had broft herr awaye yf hitt hadd nott bynne for the number of botys that laye under the Frenche mannys foreship.'

The Scots then mounted on the shore two pieces of brass and ten large iron pieces of artillery, and so drove off the pinnace and her boat. The ship was towed into harbour at high tide, to the great disappointment of Sir John Luttrell, who believed her to be laden with wine and other commodities for the Governor of Leith.

One of Luttrell's great difficulties was the want of fuel, and he was furious at the sarcastic attitude of the Scots: *I am so macchyd wythe suyche stobborne neyhbors that yf I be a colde, they gyve me leve [to] blowe my fyngers, whose gentylnes, as I maye, I shall ryght well accquytt, and the better whenseover hitt shall please the Councell tapoynt me wherwytheall.* In another letter, he says: *I have bynne dryvenn to burne too botys, to cutt downe and byrne 2 or thre lytell treys thatt grew aboute the howse, and yett yn thend have benn fayne to goo to the Fyfe syde to scyrmyshe wythe them for to gett owte some of theyr botes to burne, wher I have lost 2 of my menn.*

On the arrival of an English ship, the Scots withdrew, and Sir John Luttrell sent away all the pioneers, keeping only a few artificers to make doors, iron work and walls to support platforms, and some very 'simple' soldiers.

In November, Lord Grey of Wilton ordered the master of ordnance at Newcastle to send certain specified munitions to Inchcolm, but some of them got lost, and an inventory of the arms on the island describes an iron culverin as 'broken at the mouth,' and a demi-culverin as 'full of honycombes and blow,' so that 'none dare shute it'.

At the end of the month, the Council ordered that Sir John Luttrell should be reinforced and supplied with necessaries, but that he should be told to use the Double Rose for the time, to fortify the western part of the island

and to economize his powder. It was considered very doubtful whether, in the winter, provisions could be conveyed from the Tay to Inchcolm more than once a month.

Various provisions were thrown into Inchcolm in the winter, but in February 1548 it was resolved to evacuate the place, and the garrison had a stormy voyage thence to Broughty Craig on board the *Mary Hamborough*.

The *Mary Hamborough* can be seen in the background of the famous allegorical painting of Sir John Luttrell wading naked in stormy seas. His ship is struck by lightning and floundering in the tempest tossed seas while he himself throws a defiant fist that touches the left breast of a naked lady representing peace who, in turn, caresses his right arm whilst holding an olive branch.

Sir John was then made commander of a small army at the tower of Broughty Craig by the water's edge, Firth of Tay. Although he wrote that his new post 'looketh somewhat pertly over the Scots', he was soon begging for supplies of biscuits, beer, butter, horses, carts, masons and money. He wrote to Lord Somerset on 11th April 1548 pouring fourth his grievances and beginning to apportion blame as his attempts to construct a modern artillery fort became increasingly difficult:

Whereas it appeared unto me by your grace's letter addressed unto me by my brother (Thomas Luttrell) and bearing the date 22 of February that artificers (craftsmen) were commanded here at present may it please your Grace to understand that not one has arrived here as yet, beside the greatest lack of all is not yet supplied which is of victuals especially of biscuit and drink. I mean the such supplies as requested for a summer store there is yet no hope of their arrival here until the last hour, and then how the wind and passage (voyage) shall prove your Grace knows is doubtful... And the poor soldiers here are forced to such a nightly watch and daily travail and falling daily sick then consider travail of the poor men having nothing but salt meats and now rats. As for my part if it would please your grace I would rather trail the pike again as a common soldier than having this command and wanting credit.

I am sure that if your Grace knew how the poor soldiers here are discouraged with their aforesaid and misery, you would in your princely goodness pity them. They say they have served eighteen months and never had their pay which is a long time. I am, your Grace knows, but one man amongst them and notwithstanding that I have and do keep them in awe and obedience that they dare not utter their secret murmurings (discontent) and having myself the same want they have, they are content to take like pains with me, for their purse and table is both furnished as mine is, and because they see I am also a partaker of their watch and travail, they do the less complain.

Andrew Dudley, Keeper of the Jewels and Robes at Westminster and governor of Dundee, wrote in October 1547: 'Never had a man had so weak a company of soldiers given to drinking, eating and slothfulness,' although, 'the house stands well.' The town of Dundee agreed to support the garrison and resist the Governor of Scotland, Regent Arran, on 27 October 1547. The Constable of Dundee, John Scrimgeour, and the baillies and council signed the agreement, although under the duress of Dudley's two gunships.

The Earl of Argyll tried to capture the castle on 22

November 1547 and again in January 1548, with 150 men lead by the soldier Duncan Dundas, without success. Thomas Wyndham brought two more ships in December 1547 and burnt Balmerino Abbey on Christmas Day. On 12 January 1548, one hundred matchlock guns were delivered from Berwick, with powder flasks, matches, touch-boxes, and bullet moulds.

Andrew Dudley was succeeded by John Luttrell, who had been the commander at Inchcolm. On 11 May 1548, the English commander at Haddington, Grey of Wilton, wrote to Luttrell that he could not expect more supplies because of the expected French fleet. Grey also warned him of Wilton warned him against Scottish assassins in June, and Somerset required him to dismiss the German mercenaries in his command. There was some relief for Luttrell, as Lord Methven took away the guns of the Scottish counter-battery for redeployment at the Siege of Haddington on 6 June 1548.

Meanwhile Luttrell had been ordered to build a new fortification on an adjacent site. In November he wrote to Somerset describing the progress of this work, explaining that the ramparts made from turf were unstable and could not be strengthened. Luttrell said his enemies would not need guns 'for theye shall fynde hytt fallen downe redy to ther handys.' In December 1548, Patrick, Lord Gray of Foulis, was summoned to account for his treasons against the Government of Scotland, and although the French commanders argued for his execution, he was eventually pardoned at Regent Arran's command.

Thomas Wyndham and his nephew Luttrell's activities

on the Forth were called into question in November 1549, and the Earl of Rutland was required to investigate whether one of the ships they had seized was a lawful prize. On Christmas Day 1549, Mary of Guise, Mary Queen of Scot's mother, held a conference at Stirling Castle with her guests, and they agreed that more French guns could be brought to besiege Broughty. Twelve English ships arrived to support the defenders and it was 12 February 1550 before the French and Scots managed to recapture Broughty. Mary of Guise watched the successful assault on Wednesday 6 February 1550 from a vantage point across the Tay. Paul de Thermes led the French troops; 240 were injured and 50 killed.

The garrison surrendered six days later, at midnight. James Dog of Dunrobin claimed Luttrell as his prisoner and his papers were captured. His ransom of £1000 was raised on 16 May 1550 as an exchange for the sons of George Douglas of Pittendreich and the Master of Semple, who were prisoners in England (George Douglas's son would later rule Scotland as Regent Morton). Luttrell was promptly re-arrested for debts to a Dundee merchant, Robert Craig, but Regent Arran paid the merchant in September, and Luttrell was allowed home.

In June 1550, the Council at Westminster further resolved 'that Sir John Luttrell, in consideration of the notable good service he hath doone unto the Kinges Majistie during all his warres, shall have landes to the value of 100 markes by the yere during his Highnes pleasure.'

In addition, Sir John further extracted from the

government no less than £3,200 for 'the waiges of himself and his souldiours in the Northe'.

A few days after his return to Dunster Castle, certain commissioners had been empowered by the young King Edward VI to pronounce a divorce between Sir John and his wife, Mary Rice, upon proof of her adultery. It was believed Sir John had suspected this for many months and it was one of the reasons he kept asking for leave of absence whilst fighting in Scotland. But he was not the sort of man to settle down into quiet domesticity as a country squire. An encampment or the high seas were more to his liking, especially if he wished to pursue a military career. He negotiated with Thomas Wyndham, his uncle and fellow campaigner in Scotland, Henry Orchard, Sebastian Cabot's son-in-law, and John Aldey, who also served with Cabot, with a plan to go abroad in search of adventure. Captain Thomas Wyndham was to lead the expedition. He was a brave and experienced sailor, but an incorrigible pirate.

After payment of a ransom demand, prisoner of war exchange and his release from captivity in Edinburgh Castle in 1550, Sir John returned to Dunster Castle. He found that his affairs were in complete disarray and his wife's adultery caused him to apply for divorce in London. He could not settle down to domestic life, so later that year he travelled to London to organise a West African expedition to the Gold Coast with his uncle Thomas Wyndham, Sebastian Cabot and Henry Orchard. Cabot supplied the maps and charts, Orchard (Wyndham) was leader of the expedition. His venture never came to fruition, as the brave soldier succumbed to the plague.

The month of July 1551 in Greenwich, London, was miserable owing to an outbreak of the disease. Froude's History of England states:

The sufferers were in general men between thirty and forty, and the stoutest and healthiest most readily caught the infection. The symptoms were a sudden perspiration, accompanied with faintness and drowsiness. Those who were taken with full stomachs died immediately, Those who caught cold shivered into dissolution in a few hours. Those who yielded to the intense temptation to sleep, though but for a quarter of an hour, woke only to die.

A contemporary Londoner and friend of Sir John giving an account of his plight in Greenwich writes in a similar vein:

The disease began very suddenly with a sense of apprehension from Sir John, followed by cold shivers sometimes very violent, giddiness, headache and severe pains in the neck, shoulders and limbs, with great exhaustion. After the cold stage, which lasted almost three hours, followed the hot and sweating stage. The characteristic sweat broke out suddenly without any obvious cause. Accompanying the sweat, or after that was poured out, was a sense of heat, headache, delirium, rapid pulse, and intense thirst and Palpitation and pain in the heart followed. In the final stages Sir John was so exhausted he collapsed with a great desire to sleep which we thought to be fatal if he were permitted to give way to it.

But give way he did. Sir John had previously written to

the Duke of Somerset stating, 'I have in all things done my duty, I trust like a willing subject, and shall do to the death.' This declaration of loyalty forms a fitting epitaph to a brave, steadfast and resolute commander.

His uncle, Sebastian Cabot, and the rest of the crew continued with the voyage to the Gold Coast, Ivory Coast and Slave Coast on the Gulf of Benin, bringing back 'treasures that delighted all of London'.

This then was the pioneering adventure that English sailors such as Drake were to follow during the reign of Elizabeth 1 with such success that the monopoly of Spain and Portugal on the oceans of the world would be broken.

Captain Thomas Wyndham led a further piratical expedition with three ships in 1553 to West Africa, but died of fever on a river estuary in Benin.

Somerset and the Spanish Armada

The root cause of the Spanish 'Invincible Armada' lay in events more than forty years before. In 1587 Mary, Queen of Scots, was executed in England on the orders of Queen Elizabeth. In 1544 Sir John Luttrell of Dunster Castle had been involved in Henry VIII's ambitions to unite the kingdoms of Scotland and England by a 'treaty' and the marriage of the young Mary to his son, Prince Edward, later Edward VI. But these negotiations came to nothing and instead Scotland allied itself with France, having endured the 'rough wooing' by England for six years. However Edward became seriously ill and died in 1553. His successor was Mary I, later known as 'Bloody Mary', daughter of Catherine of Aragon, and she married Philip of Spain and wanted to restore England to the Catholic faith.

During Mary's five-year reign 275 Protestants had been put to death for refusing to revert back to Catholicism. On the accession of Elizabeth I in 1558 England was restored to the Protestant faith, which incensed Philip of Spain. The final straw was the execution of Mary Queen of Scots at Fotheringhay Castle, near Peterborough, Northamptonshire in 1587. Mary was a Catholic, and Philip II believed he had a duty to ensure no more Catholics were arrested in England and that no more should be executed. Mary had also made it clear that if she became Queen of England, Philip should inherit the throne after her death. Hence his decision to attack and invade England.

Although there was no invasion along Somerset's coastline, records from Queen Elizabeth and her ministers did not rule this out and extensive preparations were made and orders given to George Luttrell to carry out defensive precautions along his coastline. Even during the reign of Henry VIII, measures were in place to defend 'The Coste of England upon Severn'. So guns were placed at the mouth of the Parret at Burnham on Sea; a battery below Minehead (North Hill) and semi-circular enclosures of piles off Watchet and Porlock. At Hurlestone point and Porlock village itself, two round towers were built. From George Trevelyan's archives at Nettlecombe Court we now know that just before the Armada sailed elaborate precautions were taken to 'impeach a hostile landing'.

Nettlecombe oaks once provided tall strong trees for shipbuilding. During the reign of Queen Elizabeth I, timber hewn from the oaks of Nettlecombe and from special places on the Brendon hills near Dunster Castle, were hand-selected to help build the ships of the English fleet commanded by Sir Walter Raleigh which defeated the Spanish Armada. A number of other English ships that sailed the world to establish Britain's colonies and its navy and trading empire were built of prime Nettlecombe oaks.

In each parish on the Quantock and Brendon Hills men were ready to assemble under leaders such as George Luttrell and George Trevelyan and to 'repair at a moment's notice to any danger spot seen on the coast'. Careful watch along the sea was kept at Cleeve Hill above Watchet, with a system of fire-signalling to the Quantocks at such places as 'fire-beacon hill' above Crowcombe and on to Bagborough (known as the Beacon borough).

Many hills in Somerset still bear the name Beacon Hill, and most if not all of these came into the warning system, which was carefully planned and under the control of the Justices of the Peace to ensure that no false alarm and consequent confusion could take place. Evidence of this has survived in a document giving details of the arrangements made in the western parts of the county, in the Hundred of Williton and Freemanors, in preparation for defence against the possibility of a French landing in 1555, when Mary I was Queen of England.

It appears that the coastal beacons (three are mentioned, at Porlock, ie Selworthy, Cleeve Hill near Watchet and Beacon Hill on the Western end of the Quantocks) were each to have three beacon fires. These were probably of the usual pattern of that time, a brazier or iron fire-basket on a large metal tripod, and were filled with dry combustible material, well soaked in tar or pitch, ready to blaze up when ignited with flint and steel or by a burning match from a lanthorn. The signal code consisted of one fire as preliminary warning of danger, two fires for an imminent invasion and all three as the final emergency when the enemy had landed.

Collinson, the eighteenth-century historian of Somerset, describes the remains at Dunkery Beacon on Exmoor, the highest point (1705 feet) in all Somerset, with 'three large fire-hearths about eight feet square and built of rough unwrought stones. The fire-places form an equilateral triangle'. The inner line of beacons in this area consisted of sites with two beacon fires and a code of signals depending on the coastal warnings.

There might have been more of the enemy ships, with a larger complement of sailors and soldiers, had not Sir Francis Drake, in April 1587, attacked those that were then assembled in the harbour of Cadiz and sunk at least a hundred men-of-war and transports filled with supplies. During thirty-six hours, in the port of Cadiz, Drake, this most gallant and audacious of the 'Sea-Kings of Devon', burned and ravaged and plundered, after which he carried destruction to the fishing fleets along the Spanish coasts upon which the enemy depended for much of their provisions. Having so daringly 'singed the King of Spain's whiskers,' as he gaily termed this wonderful sea-foray, Drake returned triumphantly to England, carrying with him the stirring tidings and heartening his countrymen for the inevitable conflict before them.

Almost every outstanding hilltop could be used as a beacon, and many were ready prepared for use during times of emergency. At Crook Peak, on Mendip, the parish of Banwell maintained a beacon ready for firing long before the Armada sailed. The Churchwardens' Accounts for 1580 include a payment of five shillings for a 'load of wood for the Beaken and for carrying the same to Croke peke'. But beacons were dependent on fine weather for visibility, and one wonders how far away the fires could be seen at times of mist or cloud. This may account for the fact that in some parts of the county beacons were sited fairly close together. The range of the Quantock Hills, only about eight miles from end to end, included beacons at almost every high point, some not much more than a mile apart. At Ilminster, Beacon Hill to the north of the town is only 337 feet above sea-level, yet it must have served as a link in the main chain of communication by fire signal to give warning over the moors of West Somerset. Dundon, near Glastonbury, at exactly the same height as the Ilminster Beacon, commands a wide view of Sedgemoor and provided a link with the Mendip Hills at Beacon Hill above Shepton Mallet. From here could be seen the Dorset and Wiltshire beacons.

Elizabeth I was well informed of the preparations made and knew that this part of her coastline, defended by men like George Sydenham of Combe Sydenham, Colonel Luttrell of Dunster Castle, Sir John Stowell of Cothlestone Manor, and many others, both 'pikemen' and 'shotmen', were ready to receive the Spanish enemy.

Upwards of twelve thousand men were recruited in Somerset and at Minehead there were two ships, one of thirty-five tons and the other at forty-six tons. There is also evidence in State papers to show that Somerset and South Wales were grouped in one command. There were even plans and projects for a Spanish Armada working from Milford Haven, should it have fallen to the Spaniards, to make a descent upon the north coast of Somerset between Minehead and Bridgwater. French and Spanish invasions along this part of the channel was held to be likely for centuries, and with good reason, so the coast-alarms that filled Somerset and South Wales were kept alive.

The beacons would be of little value if there were no defenders ready to resist the invaders. At this time there was no regular army, so preparations had to be made locally to have men trained. In 1547 an order was issued throughout the whole country 'to have ready a good number of able horse and foot, either for the annoyance of our enemies or the defence of the realm'. In the early years of the reign of Elizabeth I, when the threat of invasion was increasing, more detailed preparations were made. Commissioners were appointed for each county, those for Somerset including Sir John Wyndham, George Luttrell, Sir George Speke, Henry Portman and John Horner, who prepared a list of 'able' men - not professional soldiers, but fit and ready to be trained to fight. Musters were held at intervals, as the danger of invasion increased, to check the numbers of the men available, the quality of their arms and their readiness for action. All owners of large estates had to provide horses and horsemen with equipment for fighting, the numbers depending on the size of the estate. The lists are long and include finally, just before the Armada sailed, 800 men with guns, 700 bowmen, 500 men with pikes or bills and 1000 other armed men. A further reserve of 1000 men had also received some training. Coastal defences were prepared, and the possible landing places at Porlock, Minehead, Watchet, Bridgwater, Axbridge and Bristol were specially protected with trenches and parapets. Pits were to be dug and ramparts built to 'empeach' a landing. All bridges and fords were to be guarded, and stores of gunpowder and arms were set up in the towns.

The success of the whole undertaking depended on the quickness of the response to the first warnings, so the beacons of the coastal counties were of special importance. During periods of training there had been some confusion, but, in March 1588, the Muster Master could report before leaving Somerset for Wiltshire: 'I have viewed and trayned the numbers bothe of foot and horse twyce since my cominge into this Countie of Somerset and... I fynde them brave and verye well furnished especially the pickes and shott whereof there are manie muskets. The trewthe is it is a moste gallaunte countrey for the men, armour and redines.'

The 4000 men returned as trained were organised into five regiments of 800 men each. Each regiment had its complement of gunners, archers and billmen, as well as heavily armed lancers and light horsemen. There were carriages for gunpowder, match and bullets, with pioneers in charge of them.

In addition to all this, Somerset, as a maritime county, was expected to help with the navy. All ships and mariners were to be 'impressed' in emergency, food was to be at hand to provision ships, and the larger ports were to send ships of above 40 tons to assist the navy. In Somerset, Taunton and Chard helped to furnish a ship from Lyme Regis. Only Bridgwater among the Somerset ports was of sufficient size to send a ship, and the 'William' with 40 men was ordered to join Drake's division at Plymouth. Nothing is known of the part played by this tiny ship in the fight against the Armada.

Though Somerset was involved in the coastal warnings it was not called into action, for the Armada passed up the English Channel far out of sight of the watchers on the Somerset, Devon and Dorset beacons. The first sightings were from the coast of Hampshire and the beacons were fired. From Dorset 3000 men marched into Hampshire to help to protect Portsmouth, and to replace them a similar number of men went from Somerset to Dorset. This, as far as is known, is all the county was called on to do while the enemy was actually in sight in the Channel. A further 4000 men were sent from Somerset to London, but little is known about them except the record of their return in August when the danger had passed.

So Somerset, like Devon and Dorset, was spared the alarm and action which came to the coastal counties from Hampshire to Kent. The greatest burden fell upon Kent and from Dover to Gravesend, every man was ready for action, but no enemy was either destined or allowed to land except as a prisoner.

CHAPTER TWELVE

The English Civil War

The siege and surrender of Dunster Castle

With the Proceedings against Dunster Castle, the manner of the enemies marching out, and our marching in, and settling thereof being the true copies of the originals, published according to order of Parliament." - Lord Fairfax, Parliamentary General, 22nd April 1646, B.M. British Library. The above was the title of a report written by Sir Thomas Fairfax, Commander of the New Model Army, to the House of Commons in London on how the six-month siege had ended at Dunster Castle, and of Parliament's other victories in the west.

The English Civil War started in 1642 when King Charles I raised his royal standard in Nottingham. The split between Charles and Parliament was such that neither side was willing to back down over the principles that they held and war was inevitable as the only way all problems could be solved. The country was split, as indeed was the county of Somerset, into those who supported the King and those who supported Parliament – all the classic ingredients for a civil war.

Towns and villages alike in Somerset suffered depredations as soldiers on both sides committed wanton destruction and took over country houses at will. A lawyer, John Turbevill, summed up the situation in a letter where he stated that his house 'is and hath been full of soldiers this fortnight, such uncivil drinkers and thirsty souls that a barrel of good beer trembles at the sight of them, and the whole house nothing but a rendezvous of tobacco and spitting.'

As with most wars during the 17th century, the English Civil War was not long and continuous. Armies lacked mobility, and the time taken to collect the most basic of equipment meant that there were long periods when no fighting was taking place. The weather was a major determining factor in whether armies could fight or not, especially in West Somerset. Roads were no more than tracks and the winter could cut them up to put them beyond use. Moving armies around would be very difficult, but Dunster Castle had a commanding and strategic role to play as guardian of sea route to the King's forces further north, and therefore was a prize worth taking and holding.

In fact the counties of Gloucestershire, Somerset and Wiltshire were all of prime importance during the Civil War for the supply of food, uniforms and munitions. The area also controlled vital routes by road and river and the three lucrative ports of Bristol, Minehead and Gloucester.

In July 1642, King Charles commissioned the Marquis of Hertford, Lieutenant- General of the six south west counties of Hampshire, Dorset, Wiltshire, Somerset, Devon and Cornwall, and sent him from Oxford into the south west with a Commission of Array and orders to rally support for the Royalist cause. It wasn't long before the conflict began in earnest in Somerset.

The first shots in the English Civil War were fired at Marshall's Elms, near Street in Somerset, when the Royalists attempted to recruit support in the area, while the Parliamentary committee were meeting only six miles to the east at Shepton Mallet. Early in August 1642, a small Royalist force of about 80 horse moving from Wells towards Burrow Bridge to bar the crossing of the Parrett met and defeated a body of Parliamentary recruits of more than 600 men. Seven Parliamentarians were killed on the spot and eighteen died later from wounds. So the first blood had been shed in this part of the country, and from then on it was open war between Royalist and Parliament in the West. News of this skirmish soon reached Dunster Castle, which was then held for parliament, and the garrison was put on high alert.

Later, however, the castle was held by the Royalist MP for Minehead and Captain of the Kings Horse, Col Francis Wyndham, close cousin of Thomas Luttrell, from June 1643 until April 1646, when it surrendered to the commander of the Taunton Garrison, Col. Robert Blake, backed up by a regiment from the New Model Army.

In 1642 the enraged Earl of Bedford, commanding for Parliament, at once issued warrants for the apprehension of any of the Marquis of Hertford's men. He sent off posts to 'Master' Luttrell at Dunster Castle to 'strengthen and make good his castle there'. Luttrell quickly and readily obeyed, increasing his garrison by one hundred men. Anticipating that the Royalists would try to cross over to Wales when they arrived in Minehead, he ordered rudders to be removed from all ships in the harbour.

The Marquis duly arrived in Minehead and fortified himself in a 'strong Inn', and then, under his Lieutenant General, Sir Ralph Hopton, rode to Dunster and attempted to gain possession of Dunster Castle, barely a mile away. Sixty Cavaliers were sent to there to demand entry, a demand that was immediately and imperiously denied. After a brief conversation and further attempts to gain entry 'Mistresse' Luttrell commanded her soldiers within to 'give fire', a command which the Royalist officer told the defenders not to obey, but Jane Luttrell, now furious, again commanded them 'upon their very lives to do it', which they did with purpose. To be fired upon from behind strong castle ramparts was more than these Cavaliers expected, and they wheeled around and beat a hasty retreat. So the first shots in West Somerset were fired by forces for Parliament manning Dunster Castle.

Although the Royalists eventually managed to escape in coal ships to Wales, the inhabitants of both Minehead and Dunster were fearful of them returning by surprise and gaining possession of the castle, from which it was considered that 10,000 men would not be able to dislodge them. Sir Ralph Hopton was accused by his commander, the Marquis of Hertford, of cowardice before the enemy. The Marquis wrote to King Charles I informing him of the disastrous encounter with 'Mistresse' Luttrell at the gates of Dunster Castle and said that had it not been for his 'owne Horse and Foot we had lost our ordnance, hazarded our persons, and lost the honour of that daye's work'.

To this Sir Ralph Hopton replied in a letter: 'May it please your Lordship, with humble pardon, according to my weake ability I have considered you worthy advertisements and vindicate myself and country from your Lordship's mistake. First whereas you condemned our endeavours and cowardly behaviour at Minehead and Dunster, your Lordships command had good success considering the great odds of five to one (at Dunster Castle)'.

Early in January 1643, Royalist Welshmen gave trouble on the coast of Somerset. Some of them blockaded Minehead harbour, and by preventing the entry of any ships or boats, stopped the supply of provisions and coal. Others, about five hundred in number, under Captain Paulet, landed there, 'invaded' the county, and 'constrained the inhabitants to yeeld to any taxation and to submit themselves servants and slaves to every poor, base companion, to save their throats from being cut.'

This party made an attack upon Dunster Castle, but Thomas Luttrell, being prepared, was able to repulse them and secure the town from plunder. When a shot from the Castle killed some of the assailants, Captain Paulet was moved to wrath and vowed that he would quarter the murderer and hang his limbs on the battlements as food for ravens. In fact he moved on to Barnstaple, with two hundred musketeers and forty horsemen.

In May 1643, we find Thomas Luttrell using a pass for his niece Margaret Trevelyan to cross over to Wales, and he afterwards promised to assist her husband, George Trevelyan of Nettlecombe Court, if he would compound for his delinquency and not persist in his 'former disobedience unto the Parliament.' The Trevelyan family were staunch Royalist and this shows how family and friends were bitterly divided as men fought for King or Parliament.

On the part of George Trevelyan of Nettlecombe there was no hesitation. He was the eldest son of the eighth John Trevelyan, and of Margaret, daughter of George Luttrell. In August 1642 he was promoted to the charge of an independent troop, and on the 22nd March 1643 he was authorised to raise a regiment of twelve hundred foot for the King. Another cousin of the Luttrells, Col Francis Wyndham, was to command the castle until its eventual surrender in 1646.

In April 1640, Wyndham had been elected Member of Parliament for Minehead in the Short Parliament. Francis Wyndham became a colonel in the army of Charles I and was engaged in the defence of Bridgwater Castle as well as Dunster Castle. After the Battle of Worcester in 1651, Wyndham was instrumental in the escape of Charles II to France, hiding him in his house at Trent, Dorset for several days.

When military operations seemed for the time more favourable to the Royalist cause, Thomas Luttrell began to have doubts as to the wisdom of the course that he had pursued, and Francis Wyndham was able to report that he 'found good inclinations in him' to deliver up his castle, although he was 'much distracted and disturbed' by some persons near him, the most powerful of whom was doubtless his wife.

Eventually, with a fine of one thousand pounds, the castle was surrendered and garrisoned for King Charles. Jane Luttrell had earlier been the Jane Popham who scattered a force of Royalists early in September 1642, by cannon fire.

Clarendon relates that, in the middle of June 1643, the Marquess of Hertford obtained possession of Taunton and Bridgewater in three days, and continues:

Dunster Castle, so much stronger than both the other that it could not have been forced, yet by the dexterity of Francis Windham, who wrought upon the fears of the owner and master of it, Mr. Lutterel, was, with as little bloodshed as the other, delivered up to the King; into which the Marquis put in him that took it as Governor, as he well deserved.

Thomas Luttrell was moreover compelled to pay a large sum, either as a fine or as proof of devotion to the Royalist cause. There is in the Morning Room at Dunster Castle a significant receipt as follows:

xxiijto die Junii 1643. Received the day and yeare above written to his Majesties use by me Edward Kyrton, Esq. Treasurar for the army under the comaund of the right honorable the Marquesse of Hertford, Liftenant Generall of his

Majesties forces in the west, of Thomas Luttrell of Dunstar Castle in the county of Somerset, Esq. the summe of five hundred powndes, in part of payment of the summe of one thousand powndes which the said Mr. Luttrell is to pay towardes the charge of the said army. I say receaved, Edw. Kyrton.

Whether Thomas Luttrell remained in his own castle is not stated. He died a few months later, and was buried there on the 7th of February 1644. In the castle's Inner Hall there is a portrait on panel dating from the later part of the reign of James the First, which represents this Thomas Luttrell. The subject of it has long hair and a short beard. He is attired in a light green doublet and trunk hose, with a falling collar edged with lace, and white cuffs. He has a black hat under his right arm and a sword under the other.

Within a few days of the death of Thomas Luttrell, his relict was compelled to pay a large sum to the Crown, as appears by the following receipt:

13th February 1643. Then received of Mrs. Jane Luttrell the summe of fiveteene hundred pounds, as soe much due to his Majestie for the fyne of her selfe and her two sonnes; I say received for his Majestie's service the day and yeere above written the summe of 1500, by me Francis Hawley.

The two sons mentioned were George and Francis Luttrell. The person who gave it was merely an officer in the Royalist Army, but the payment might possibly be regarded as the purchase money for the wardship of the heir of the Dunster estate, who was a minor at the time of the death of his father. A few weeks later, there is another acquittance:

25to die Marcii 6144, anno regni Regis Caroli 190. Receaved then of Mistriss Jane Luttrell the summe of three score pownds in parte of payment of one hundred pownds which she was to pay by way of loane upon His Majestie's lettre in the nature of a privie seale for His Majestie's service. I say reaceaved. Per me William Prowse, deput' vicecomitis.

Jane Luttrell must have been furious at having to supply money for the party which she and her relations had so steadily opposed and despised. In later and happier times, she lived at Marshwood, near Blue Anchor, and the house, now a farmhouse, still stands to this day. Jane died in 1668 and was buried in St George's Church, Dunster that November.

George Luttrell, son and successor of Thomas, was baptized at Dunster on the 12th of September 1625. Nothing is known about his early years, but it may safely be assumed that his mother would not have allowed him to go to Oxford to mix with young Cavaliers. At the time of his father's death, Dunster Castle was occupied by a Royalist garrison, and the manor house at East Quantoxhead was in the possession of Lady Skory, no friend to the Luttrells. A smaller house at Marshwood was, however, available for the widow and her children.

'With the Proceedings against Dunster Castle, the manner of the enemies marching out, and our marching in, and settling thereof being the true copies of the originals, published according to order of Parliament' stated Sir Thomas Fairfax, Parliamentary General and Commander of the New Model Army. The above was the title of a report to the House of Commons in London on how the six-month siege of Dunster had ended, and of Parliament's other victories in the west. The siege, plague and pestilence had its origins three years after the Royalists took command.

In the middle of May 1645, Charles I gave orders that the Prince of Wales, future Charles II, should take up his residence for a while at Dunster Castle to 'encourage the new levies,' but it was not known to him, nor at Court, that the plague, which had driven him from Bristol, was 'as hot in Dunster town, just under the walls of the Castle.'

St George's Church parish register records the burial of no fewer than eighty persons at Dunster in that month. Two of them are described as soldiers, from which it may be inferred that the Castle itself, isolated from the town beneath it, was not free from the prevailing sickness. At nearby Minehead the death rate in 1645 was about five times that of a normal year.

The inhabitants of a long street in Dunster are said to have established communications between their respective houses by making openings in the party walls 'so as to avoid all necessity of going into the open street', whose air was dangerous to life. There had been a previous outbreak of the plague not too long before this one and it was so serious that charitable aid from other parts of the country were called for, possibly by George Luttrell, who had been High Sheriff of Somerset at the time.

The plague repeatedly returned to haunt English cities, towns and villages from the 13th to the 17th century. No one was immune. In many places it was claimed that the dead exceeded the living. Symptoms of infection included swollen, tender lymph nodes, high fever, chills and haemorrhages under the skin, causing blackish discolouration of the skin, hence the common name of Black Death. Dunster may very well have had its own Pest House for plague victims and Plague Pits for communal plague burials.

This then was the Prince of Wales' environment for two weeks during May 1645.

The Prince, who was then just fifteen years of age, occupied a small room within the room at the south-western end of the Gallery in Dunster Castle (traditionally known as King Charles' Room). After about a fortnight, he proceeded to Barnstaple. The churchwarden's accounts of Minehead for this year contain the following entries:

Given the ringers in beere at severall tymes when the Prince and other great men came into the towne, 14s... Paid the Prince's footman, which he claymed as due to him for his fee, 5s. 6d.

At that juncture it might have been imprudent to ignore the Prince's visit. Less than four months afterwards there is an entry in the same book which reflects more faithfully the state of public opinion at Minehead: *Paid the ringers when Bristoll was taken, 3s.*

After the reverses of the Royalist party at Langport, Taunton and Bridgewater in the summer of 1641, Dunster

Castle remained the only place held for the King in Somerset. Being isolated, it was harmless except as a source of annoyance to the immediate neighbourhood.

In early January 1646, rumours flew that the castle had been relieved. There were also claims that during the skirmish Parliamentary forces had taken Col Wyndham's mother prisoner and sent in their last summons to surrender, 'If you will yet deliver up the Castle, you shall have faire quarter, if not, expect no mercy; your mother shall be placed in front, to receive the first fury of your cannon: we expect your answer.' Col Wyndham reputedly shouted at Col Blake that this was 'the most barbarous and villainous act that was ever done', yet he refused to surrender the castle, asking his mother's forgiveness and stating that the rebels would answer for the spilling of her blood. The Parliamentary party in London denounced this report as a 'feeble lie' and 'ale-house intelligence', but continued a propaganda war by accusing the castle of consorting with papists, breaking the Sabbath with ungodly pastimes and having several 'priests of Baal' within its walls.

The continuation of the siege drew unwanted attention towards Dunster, so Col Blake was ordered to spring the mines which had been dug under the walls on the north-east side (the Barbican wall between the Gatehouse and mansion), fully expecting to blow up the castle. Knowing of these mines however, the garrison had already discovered one and intercepted it. The second either did not fire or did not spring, whilst the third exploded, destroying part of the Barbican and causing a considerable breach; luckily the road opened by the explosion proved so inaccessible and steep that the intended attack could not be made. To the defenders, however, now very short of necessities, the breach proved a great annoyance, as they were put to double duty to keep their guards.

In this emergency, Sir Richard Grenville wrote to Colonel Wyndham exhorting him to hold out yet a little longer and promising that help should certainly be sent. Two regiments accordingly set out on the 8th of January, ostensibly to relieve Exeter, but really destined for Dunster Castle. Their plan was either betrayed or discovered by their opponents, for some horse and foot were called from their winter quarters to watch them, and if necessary to go and strengthen Colonel Blake. Seeing that their enemy was thus prepared and that relief was impossible, the Royalists once more retired, and the blockade of Dunster was continued without interruption until the end of January.

On 5th February 1646 the Royalist forces managed to enter the castle to deliver four barrels of powder, thirty cows and fifty sheep. When they were inside, the Royalists then spoilt several more of Col Blake's mines which had been laid under the western curtain walls by miners from the Mendips, and destroyed the earthworks thrown up by the besiegers. When the Royalists left for Barnstaple, Blake sallied forth from the Ship Inn (now the Luttrell Arms Hotel) and took the men prisoner.

Around midday on Friday 17th April, Colonel Blake of Taunton Garrison with their regiment, bolstered by

Major-General Skipton's regiment, drew up in two bodies dressed in full battle array on May Hill; the men numbered two thousand strong and were in full view of the beleaguered castle garrison. Col Blake sent in the final summons for surrender. Deprived of all hope of relief, Col Wyndham demanded a 'parley'. The castle was surrendered on 19th April 1946, after having sustained a siege of about 160 days and the loss of 20 men, in the knowledge that their water supply was about to be poisoned. Col Wyndham negotiated an honourable surrender which allowed the beleaguered garrison to march out with drums beating, arms shouldered, bullets between their teeth, match lit at both ends, flags flying high and prisoners on both sides released with safe passage for those soldiers who wished to join the King at Oxford.

The full terms and conditions of the surrender of Dunster Castle were as follows:

1. *That the Castle, together with the armes ammunition, and other ferniture of war (except what is hereunder excepted), be delivered up into the hands of the said Colonel Blake for his Exellency Sir Thomas Fairfax, to the use of the King and Parliament.*

2. *That all Commissioners Officers in the Castle shall march away with horses and armes and all other necessary accounterments appertaining.*

3. *That common officers and souldiers, both horse and foot, shall march away with their armes and either horse or foot souldier shall have three charges of powder and bullet, with*

three yards of match, for those that have matchlocks, together with colours and drums.

4. *That the said Colonel Wyndham shall carry with him all that is properly his, and that which doth properly belong to the Lady Windham shall be sent to her.*

5. *That all officers and souldiers with all particular persons of the Castle shall march forth secure, as many as will, to Oxford without delay, and those who are otherwise minded shall lay down their armes and have Let-passes to their homes, or to any other places they shall desire with protection against the violence of the soldiers.*

6. *That prisoners to either party be released.*

7. *That the said Colonel Francis Windham and his souldiers march to Oxford in twelve daies.*

An honourable surrender indeed for the Royalists in Dunster Castle, but Parliament was now in full control of the whole county. When the Roundhead army marched into Dunster Castle, six pieces of ordnance and two hundred stand of arms were all the booty found within its walls, reputedly along with a score of dead rats and a scattering of chicken and other animal bones.

During the siege Col Blake made his headquarters at the Ship Inn. His main field artillery and gun emplacements were on the high ridge of the Old Deer Park (above the present day car park), with further cannon lines between what is now the car park and the river Avil. Roundhead positions were at Lawns Bridge (the closest position to the castle), Galloxbridge, Frackford and Loxhole Bridge, with Parliamentary troops in position on May Hill, opposite the castle, with clear views of the Royalist garrison. Soldiers were also stationed on a rising piece of ground on Ducky Path Plantation below Grabbist Hill. Surrounded on all sides and with news of Royalists defeats all over the country, it is not surprising that Col Wyndham chose to capitulate.

Blake had joined the Parliamentary Army of Sir John Horner and become a captain in Alexander Popham's regiment. At the defence of Bristol in 1643, he earned a reputation as a determined fighter. He fought on after the parliamentary commander Fiennes had surrendered the city and Prince Rupert, the Royalist commander, was minded to hang him. Promoted to Lieutenant Colonel, he was sent to defend Lyme against the Royalist army of Prince Maurice. Though not the senior officer, it was Blake who directed the stubborn defence of the town, which saw off far superior numbers.

Blake moved on to Taunton in the late spring of 1644 to raise a new regiment for parliament. The new regiment, in turn, was despatched to join the army of the Earl of Essex, leaving Blake as Governor of the town with a makeshift force of 1,000. Between October 1644 and July 1645, Taunton endured three sieges, successively blockaded by Edmund Wyndham, Governor of Bridgwater, Sir John Berkley and Lord Goring. By the end of his heroic defence of Taunton, the town, with the exception of the castle, was all but destroyed and the people were starving, but the news had made Blake a hero in London.

Colonel Blake, writing from Taunton on the 21st of April to report the event to the Parliament, remarked that, at the price of time and blood, he could no doubt have obtained very different terms, but that he was induced to accept these by his wish to follow the exemplary clemency of his general. 'The place,' he said, was 'strong and of importance for the passage into Ireland.' A public thanksgiving was now ordered in London for the many and continued successes of the Parliamentary forces, Dunster Castle being named in the list of places whose capture deserved especial emphasis.

Minehead, too, rejoiced that her disagreeable neighbour had fallen, and 'paid the ringers when Dunster Castle was yeelded up' four shillings and eight pence. A few of Blake's cannonballs have been unearthed on the Tor in recent years. His principal battery was, it is believed, behind the house now called the Luttrell Arms Hotel. Another may have been on the north side of the town, as in the 19th century a ball, presumably fired by the defenders of the Castle, was found in the roof of the church.

John Question of Dunster, surgeon, was in 1647 subjected to a fine of £100 for espousing the Royalist cause, but the amount was eventually reduced to £10 in consideration of the gratuitous services which he had rendered to sick and hurt soldiers serving under Colonel Blake during the siege.

With the surrender of Dunster Castle the fighting ceased

in Somerset and the whole county fell under obedience to Parliament. The war was now virtually over. The Royalists, defeated everywhere, were soon disbanded, and the King, now a captive, was detained in prison till the bitter end. He was put on trial and executed on 30th January 1649, and on the 6th February that year, the monarchy was abolished. Parliament stated that 'the office of the king in this nation is unnecessary, burdensome and dangerous to the liberty, society and public interest of the people.'

Oliver Cromwell's name appears third in the list of 26 MPs in the 'Rump Parliament' which voted for the king's execution. What became known as a Council of State was set up instead of a monarchy. Oliver Cromwell was its first chairman.

A Roundhead garrison was maintained at Dunster Castle for more than five years after its surrender. In October 1649, some nine months after the King's execution, it was proposed to place 2,000 foot (footsoldiers) of Somerset in Dunster Castle. On the 25th March 1650 Cromwell's Council of State resolved:

That it be referred to the Committee which confers with the Officers of the Armie to consider whether or noe Dunster Castle and Taunton Castle, or either of them, are fit to be demolished, and to report their opinions therein.

On 16th May, twelve barrels of gunpowder were issued 'for the supply of Taunton and Dunster Castle,' and later that month a further demand of the Governor of Dunster Castle for arms and ammunition was referred to the Committee of the Ordnance.

The following resolutions determine the state of Dunster Castle's historical defences as we see them to this day. They were entered in the order-book of the Council of State for the year 1650:

6 June: That a letter bee written to Colonell Desbrow, to let him know that this Councell leaves it to him to put in such number of men into Dunster and Taunton Castles as hee shall thinke fit to secure them.

5 August: That it bee refered to the Committee which meets with the Officers of the Armies to take into consideration the present condition of Dunster Castle, and to reportto the Councel their opinions what they thinke fitt to bee done therein, either as to the making it untenable or repairing of its.

10 August: At the Committee for Marshall Affaires. Ordered that the Committee, having seriously considered the present state of the guarrison at Dunster Castle, and finding that the making of it every way teneable against an enemy will require a great summe of money which they conceive the Councell at present cannot well spare, conceive it necessary that the said guarrison be drawne to Taunton, and that the Castle be soe farre slighted as that it may not be made suddainely teneable by an enemy, and that it be referred to Major General Desbrow to the Commissioners of the Militia for the county to see this done and to send an account thereof to the Council.

The work of destruction was set in hand without delay, a rate being levied in Somerset 'for pulling downe Dunster Castle'. A communication written on the spot on the 27th of August says:

Here hath been above two hundred men working at this Castle these twelve daies about sleighting the same, which is almost finished except the dwelling-house of Mr. Luttrell and the Gatehouse, according to order of the Council of State.

However, on 20th August a resolution was made by the Council of State to halt the demolition. Unfortunately it arrived seven days too late to save most of the medieval defence structures:

To write to Major Robinson that Dunster Castle be continued in the condition it is till further order of the Councell, and that there be twenty or thirtie chozen (sic) *there for the defence thereof.*

Dunster Castle may well have looked different had those orders arrived in time, with the prison and granary tower, curtain walls, wing walls and perhaps the Shell Keep still preserved. The twenty or thirty soldiers were billeted in what are now known as the castle's Morning Room and Leather Gallery, whose early 17th century floorboards are still to be seen and walked on to this day.

CHAPTER THIRTEEN

The Pitchfork Rebellion and the Battle of Sedgemoor

Anyone who is Somerset-born or who has lived for long in the county will have a special interest in and feeling for the Monmouth 'affair', the Protestant rising led by James, Duke of Monmouth and bastard son of Charles II against the Roman Catholic James II in 1685, which led to defeat and disaster at Sedgemoor for the Duke, the last pitched battle ever fought on English soil. The story of the rising and its aftermath, the Bloody Assize - the trial of hundreds of the defeated rebels at Dorchester, Exeter, Taunton, Wells and other towns of the South West - and the conviction and execution of a large number and the transportation of most of the remainder has remained one of the most vivid and moving incidents in the history of Somerset.

Most of the rebels were everyday civilians who had taken up arms against what they saw as an unjust monarchy. Many of them were armed with nothing more than scythe blades mounted on the ends of long poles. This rag-tag army of farmers and weavers took on the might of the British army, with its muskets and plug bayonets. After a night march, in a failed attempt to surprise the enemy camp on Sedgemoor, the rebels faced volleys of musket fire and then a merciless pursuit by the king's regiments, thirsting for rebel blood.

In the Museum at Taunton we see and hear those same men writing their last letters to their loved ones, spoken by Taunton Garrison re-enactment soldiers. It is heartrending to hear the words of these condemned men as they await execution in the prison undercroft which was used to house them, having been tried by Judge Jeffries, the Hanging Judge. The judges began their work in Somerset on September 17 at Taunton, in the Great Hall of Taunton Castle, and completed their work in two days. About 500 men were brought to trial and almost all were sentenced to death, but by now it was clear that transportation was to be the fate of the majority, especially as each man transported would be worth more than £12, a source of considerable profit for the Crown,

In their final hours condemned prisoners wrote letters to loved ones and read passages from the bible. Edward Hobbes from Stogursey was High Sheriff of Somerset at the time and pulls no punches when he states:

"As Somerset's High Sheriff I had to make sure that

the execution of the prisoners was properly carried out. No detail could be overlooked. When the rebels were executed in Bath I ordered that a cauldron should be provided for boiling their heads and quarters. Some people say the punishments were barbaric. But I was just doing my job."

An example of the cauldron used to boil the mutilated rebel's corpses can also be seen in the museum.

James, Duke of Monmouth, was the illegitimate son of King Charles II. He was a charismatic and brave young man. When his father died in February 1685, Monmouth was already in exile in Holland. Many people thought he should now become king instead of his Catholic uncle, James II. Plans were quickly made for a rebellion in England, and on 11 June 1685 Monmouth landed at Lyme Regis, hoping the Protestant Westcountrymen would flock to his banner.

Francis Luttrell of Dunster Castle was appointed by the Earl of Winchilsea, Lord Lieutenant of Somerset, to be Colonel of a regiment of foot in succession to Sir Halswell Tynte, and he was in command of the local forces when the Duke of Monmouth landed at Lyme in June 1685. In this emergency he had recourse to his wife. It had been his habit to give her a guinea or broad piece of gold whenever any of his tenants paid a fine for the renewal of a lease, so she had accumulated about £500 at Dunster Castle. From this hoard she then withdrew about £200 for his assistance.

Colonel Luttrell was of course responsible for the liveries of the men in his service. The following are samples of the entries relating to them:

1683, June 26: Making of seven liveries laced, £5. Silk galloone and lineing the britches, £2. Seven pair of stockings, £1.15s. Ribbon to tye the knees, 7s.6d. Pocketts, staying tape, canvas and buckram, £1. 20 yards of gray cloath, at 10s. per yard, £10. Yellow padoway to line six coates, £3.16s. Silk to line the page's coate, 10s. Silk to make the wastcote and lineing, 18s. 6 black lacker hatts, £3. A black caster for the page, 13s. 151 yards of black and gold lace for the 7 liveries, at 6s. per yard, £45.6d. Black and gold chaine for the 7 liveries, £4.10s. Black and gold buttons for them £5.10s. Ribbons for the liveryes, £1.18s.

From other similar entries it appears that the black and gold buttons cost about 1s. 9d. per dozen, so that £5 10s.would represent about 750 buttons for the seven liveries.

Elected again for Minehead in 1685, Luttrell took no known part in James II's Parliament, but he was probably a court supporter. During the summer he commanded a militia regiment against the Duke of Monmouth, but was unable to distinguish himself as most of his men had deserted.

Despite the extravagant show of uniforms, Francis Luttrell was, however, obliged to evacuate Taunton because of desertion by men on the approach of the Duke, who there assumed the title of King and was crowned at the Market Cross by the famous 'Fair Maids of Taunton', a group of schoolgirls, who presented him with a banner.

There was a major change of plan at Taunton when Monmouth was proclaimed king. This was done to encourage the support of the country gentry. Taunton Corporation was made to witness the event at swordpoint outside the White Hart Inn. Other proclamations denounced the present Parliament as an unlawful assembly, attacked the Duke of Albemarle and opposed the payment of taxes. All these proclamations were issued in the name of the new King James, 'King Monmouth'. The Mayor of Bridgwater also proclaimed Monmouth King.

Once Monmouth's force had entered and started to fortify Bridgwater, he sent some of his cavalry to collect six cannon from Minehead. Three cannon, which could have formed part of the original six, can be seen on Minehead harbour today. Monmouth planned to stay in Bridgwater until the men returned with the cannon and then break out and head for Bristol. Feversham and his army of 500 horse and 1,500 militiamen camped on the edge of Sedgemoor at the village of Westonzoyland. Monmouth could view them from the tower of Church of St Mary in Chedzoy and may have inspected them more closely from there before deciding to attack them.

The Duke eventually led his untrained and ill-equipped troops out of Bridgwater at around 10 pm to undertake a night-time attack on the King's army. They were guided by Richard Godfrey, the servant of a local farmer, along the old Bristol road towards Bawdrip on the south side of the Polden Hills. With their limited cavalry in the vanguard, they turned south along Bradney Lane and Marsh Lane and came to the open moor with its deep and dangerous rhynes (drainage ditches).

There was a delay while the first rhyne was crossed and the first men across startled a Royalist patrol. A shot was fired and a horseman from the patrol galloped off to report to Feversham. Lord Grey of Warke led the rebel cavalry forward and they were engaged by the King's Regiment of Horse, which alerted the rest of the Royalist forces.

The superior training of the regular army and their horses routed the rebel forces by outflanking them. Grey's untrained supporters were quickly defeated by the professionals, and hundreds were cut down by cannonfire and musketfire.

Warning of Monmouth's approach was sent back to Weston, and with the call of 'Beat the drums, the enemy is come' the royal army prepared for action, hastily but without confusion. The infantry in their six battalions were quickly in position. The rebel cavalry, under Lord Grey, rode forward but failed to find the 'plungeon' or crossing over the Bussex Rhyne and were forced by the infantry fire into confusion and panic. A few tried to secure the second crossing of the rhyne but also failed.

The uncontrollable horses fled into some of the oncoming rebel infantry, adding to the confusion. Nevertheless, the rebel infantry still advanced towards the royal army, and the Dutch gunners with their little cannon caused considerable casualties among their opponents. But the infantry could not cross the rhyne, and as they grouped and fired towards the enemy, great gaps were cut in their ranks by the royal cannon. Cavalry also rode out across the plungeons as the patrols began to come in towards the sounds of battle, and with a pincer movement they attacked the main body of the rebels, who continued to fight bravely, though their leaders had decided on flight and were riding off towards the Polden Hills and Bristol.

The regular infantry had by now discovered that the Bussex Rhyne was neither deep nor difficult, so they crossed the ditch and joined the fight. The rebels were being slaughtered despite their courage, and with dawn the task began of rounding up those who had managed to escape. Aided by the Wiltshire militia, who had remained at Middlezoy (for Feversham was doubtful of their loyalty) the royal troops began the task of dealing with the prisoners - more than 200 were kept in the church - and burying the corpses left on the battlefield. The casualties are reckoned as about 400 rebels who died in the battle, with many more killed in the pursuit and rounding up of those who tried to escape, while only about 50 regular soldiers lost their lives and about 200 were wounded.

These figures can only be approximate. The main body of the army returned to its quarters, the militia were sent home, but two regiments, both from Tangier, one under Colonel Kirke - the Queen's Regiment, called Lambs from the design in their badge - remained for occupation duty and for mopping-up in the district. Their cruelty in hanging without trial men taken as prisoners earned them lasting hatred.

On the third day after the battle of Sedgemoor, the churchwardens of Dunster paid 7s. 6d. to the ringers 'upon the rout of Monmouth.' The churchwardens and the overseers alike incurred a small expense in 'presenting the rebells' at Stogumber, and three men were hanged at Dunster after the 'Bloody Assizes'.

There is in the castle at Dunster a three-quarter length portrait of a man widely believed to be the real hero of the

Royalist army. This is Peter Mews, Bishop of Winchester, named variously as 'a good old honest Cavalier', 'The Bombadier Bishop' and more commonly, 'Old Patch'. He had formerly been the Bishop of Bath and Wells and had known and been friendly with Francis Luttrell. He had returned to Somerset and Sedgemoor at the request of King James I and indeed the gentry from Somerset in 1685 to give spiritual comfort to the Royalists. Having had great experience in battle, especially at the Battle of Naseby during the English Civil War when he had served in King Charles I's devoted lifeguards, Mews quickly saw the weaknesses in the King's positions as Monmouth had attacked from the moor itself, not on the Westonzoyland to Bridgwater road, as had been expected.

Monmouth attacked the royal army camped on fields at Westonzoyland. He had found himself cornered in Bridgewater, in a hopeless position, with about 4,000 brave but inexperienced rebels. Monmouth's army were about to make a surprise attack in the middle of the night, when a shot rang out form one of his officers. According to Daniel Defoe, author of Robinson Crusoe, who was with the rebel army, it was 'fired by accident or treachery'.

When the alarm was raised the royal army found themselves unprepared. Captain Francis Compton, who had been next to the Longmoor Rhyne, ordered one of his soldiers to ride at full speed over the moor to alert the camp. He rose up and down the Bussex Rhyne, shouting 'Beat the drums, the enemy has come, for Lord's sake, beat the drum!'

Of Lord Faversham, Commander-in-Chief, there was no sign. He was fast asleep in Weston, having wined and dined with Peter Mews earlier in the day. Small wonder he was asleep at a quarter past one in the morning, when the alarm was raised. Peter Mews, on the other hand, was dressing rapidly and pulling on his breeches, hose and shoes as the alarm was repeated through the village.

By 3 am Lord Faversham had regained his senses, his valet and other servants having shaken their master awake. After a further 15 minutes he was dressed. However it was later said that he had spent a full 20 minutes preening himself before a hand glass, adjusting his cravat and combing his full bottom wig before mounting his horse and taking effective command.

In the meantime, John Churchill, second-in-command (later Duke of Marlborough and an ancestor to Winston Churchill), had organised the royal army. Although Monmouth did not have sufficient muskets for all his men, they made improvised pikes by fixing scythe blades to the long straight poles, which were described by Peter Mews and other Royalist officers as 'murderous weapons'.

However, Peter Mews was the hero of the hour, and it is only due to him that any of the royal guns got into action at Sedgemoor at all. Along with his coachman and groom, he harnessed his coach horses to the trails of a number of royal cannon and dragged them up, one at a time, from the Bridgwater road on to Sedgemoor itself. Eventually six were drawn up and placed next to the Scots Guards between the Upper and Lower Plungeons (ditch crossings). It was then that Peter Mews noticed that the guns were all levelled in the same direction, so he used his coach and horse again to draw them to another spot and place them saltire-wise (crosswise, enabling them to reach front to flank).

But still the royal gunners and civilian drivers had not arrived from Weston. Although the cannon were there, with a lack of gunners, a sergeant from the Scots regiment took over the handling of several pieces of artillery. Sergeant Weems proceeded to fire case-shot which 'made lanes amongst the enemy'.

By daybreak the Battle of Sedgemoor was almost over. Monmouth had fled the battlefield earlier, leaving behind his musketeers and scythe-men, who were now very much on their own and heavily outnumbered, because half of Monmouth's cavalry and infantry had already fled back across the moor too. Though the pitched battle had ended, the slaughter had just begun. By 7 am on the 6th July one Royalist officer was writing a letter home, adding 'our men are still killing them in the corne and hedges and ditches whither they are crept'.

On Tuesday 7th July, Col Wyndham's regiment of the Wiltshire militia set off to march home. At Glastonbury they hanged six rebels, one of them, a Lieutenant, from the sign of the White Hart Inn. The victims were stripped naked and left hanging there when the militia marched on. This was recorded by Wadham Wyndham and Adam Wheeler, drummer in the Wiltshire militia. The rebels halted at Wells for a church parade at which Peter Mews preached to them and their rebel prisoners. They hanged five of them after the service, before marching on to Norton St Philip. To many in the country Peter Mews, who had pleaded for leniency and clemency for those 'simple countrymen' who had supported Monmouth, was a hero and 'fine fellow'.

Another colourful account of the rebellion comes from West Somerset, where Francis Luttrell intended to fight for Monmouth:

It was July 1685 when Luttrell left Dunster Castle with a small army and some farm labourers to join with the Duke of Monmouth at Bridgewater. Their two cannons were extremely heavy and ale was in better supply than news of the rebel's progress. After a two week amble through the Somerset countryside visiting many local taverns along the way, the company located the Duke at Sedgemoor battlefield just as the fight was drawing to a close. When the news reached Colonel Luttrell that the Monmouth had fled the battle shortly after it had begun and his army was being massacred, he rallied his men and marched them back to Dunster, a journey completed in double quick time. The farm workers then had time to pull on their working smocks and get into the fields to be' surprised' by the news of the Kings' victory brought to them by a watchful contingent of James II troops on the look-out for fugitive rebels.

Those rebels who were caught and sentenced to death included three Dunster men, Henry Lackwell, John Geanes and William Sully. These words were marked alongside their names on the death warrant – Tr. et. ss, that is; Trahetur et Suspendaiur 'Let them be drawn and hanged'. Over three hundred were executed this way. After the hangings came the gruesome dismemberment of the corpses, burning the entrails, quartering the bodies, boiling them in salt and dipping them in pitch or tar to preserve them.

It is easy, but harrowing, to picture the scene taking place. One eyewitness account states:

The gibbets were made ready on top of a bare hill now known as Gallox Hill where in times past, many had died. After a short service in a church called St George's, the mournful procession thence passed down the West Street. These men were known to all in this village as they were surrounded by weeping relatives and friends.

They crossed an old packhorse bridge called Gallox and up to the waymarked Gallox Cross, whence they turned sharp to right and, after a steep ascent, reached the top of a bare brown hill and saw the waiting gibbets standing gaunt against grey lamenting skies.

After the hangings came the gruesome dismemberment of the corpses and the burning of their entrails. Their limbs were torn asunder, salted and boiled in pitch, this to preserve them, and their sundry parts nailed along the village High Street and on the trees along the King's highways to subdue and terrorise all those who opposed His Most Gracious Majesty.

In all this brutality surgeons like Joseph Winter from Ilchester struggled to save the lives of men, off and on the battlefield. Typical injuries inflicted include the fate of Robert Sandy who was wounded in action by 'some heavy cutting instrument to his head in two places' and the doctor's bill contains the whole gory details:

On the hinderpart of a piece of his skull was cut off and left hanging by the flesh as big as a five shilling piece and the brain left naked, only his a thin skin to keep it in, on the fore part was a large wound out of which I took several pieces of skull… but by my care he is firmly cured. The cure is honestly worth £5.

Several months after the battle we read this from *Wood's Life and Times* vol ii, p 421:

Out of a letter from Harpford dated 17 Nov. 1685, thus: — 'Lord Chief Justice (George) Jeffries said at the assize that just before the happy defeat of the rebells at Sedgmore they were reckoned to be 7000; that he thought 1000 of them were kild in the fight and about 1000 were taken since : upon which his lordship charged the country to look narrowly after the others. I cannot exactly learn how many of his majesty's forces were slaine: I think not verie many, perhaps 4 or 500. There are above 700 of those that are taken to be transported and about 40 or 50 pardoned: the rest have been executed in several places of the three counties to terrify others from doing the like hereafter.

News letter dated, S., 27 Dec. 1685 ; 'about 100 rebells in the woods neare Taunton do as yet lurk there ; build themselves tabernacles and make beds of feme: and their tabernacles are in such places that but one man can at a time come at them. They sometimes before had sallied out; went to Taunton and killed the hangman that had hanged the rebells there: some of them are taken.'

Colonel Francis Luttrell died at Plymouth on the 25th of July 1690, at the age of thirty-one, while with his regiment at Plymouth waiting to go overseas. His brother inherited his seat as well as a seriously encumbered estate, representing Minehead until his death in 1708.

Unconscious or regardless of the condition of his affairs, the widow caused his body to be removed to Dunster for interment, and so spent the then considerable sum of £300 on his funeral. The hatchment painted on this occasion is still in existence. Colonel Luttrell had four children. Several of his collection of muskets from his local militia are still to be seen at Dunster Castle, along with cannonballs dating from the English Civil War period, whilst the Battle of Sedgemoor also features in R D Blackmore's *Lorna Doone*, where the hero arrives on the battlefield as the battle is finishing and then has to go to London to face Jeffries. Another connection of note is with Daniel Defoe, who joined the Monmouth Rebellion against James II. Defoe was able to return unnoticed to London and keep out of the authorities' view until James II was displaced on the throne by William and Mary in 1689.

In the latter part of James II's reign, Col Francis was no longer a supporter. In 1687 he declined to vote for the repeal of the Penal Laws. King James had been advised by the Quaker William Penn, who believed that Protestantism was a greater danger to the country than Catholicism therefore the law should remain. Francis Luttrell was also one of the first men of importance in the West of England to join the standard of Prince William of Orange in Exeter, on the 19th November 1688.

The story of Col Francis Luttrell did not end with the

Battle of Sedgemoor, nor with his death, as his legacy lives on to this day through the original Luttrell's Foot militia raised at the castle (see appendix A).

The Wars of the Spanish Succession

Luttrells' Marines and the capture of Gibraltar

When the Green Howards, the independent regiment raised by Colonel Francis Luttrell at Dunster Castle in November 1688, were put on a regular footing, his brother Alexander received a commission to be Captain. Later, in 1702, during the reign of Queen Anne, Alexander Luttrell and his fellow brother officers accepted commissions in a regiment of Marines under the command of George Villiers. This group, later called the Luttrells' Marines (31st Foot), was one of six regiments of English marines that had been formed in preparation for the War of the Spanish Succession, or Queen Anne's War as it is sometimes called, in 1704–1713.

On the renewed outbreak of war six new Marine

Regiments were constituted under Colonels Henry Holt, Henry Mordaunt, George Villiers, Thomas Saunderson, Edward Fox and Viscount Shannon, with pay to commence as from 20 April 1702 for the privates though they were not mustered full till the 24th August. A new Establishment for them was signed on the 25 Dec. 1703 (Treasury Board Papers XC, No. 63). At the time of the capture of Gibraltar these six Regiments were under the command of Brigadier William Seymour (as succeeding Mordaunt), Alexander Luttrell (as succeeding Villiers), Holt, Fox, Saunderson and Shannon.

Queen Anne was not the first to cast an envious eye on Gibraltar's Rock. Oliver Cromwell and William of Orange had both previously shown interest, but it was her ministers who had marked it out for England. Although Gibraltar had little trading advantage and its anchorage was unprotected, its strategic value lay in the fact that England would then have control of the entrance to the Mediterranean Sea.

In January 1703, the regiment set sail for Spain in HMS *Suffolk* and HMS *Grafton* in order to join Admiral Rooke's fleet on operations in the Mediterranean. Unfortunately on 6th December 1703, Colonel Villiers was drowned off Malta; he was succeeded by his Lieutenant-Colonel, Alexander Luttrell. The name of the regiment was duly changed to reflect their new leader and the Luttrell Marines continued to Gibraltar, intending to furnish landing parties and to provide small arms fire for close-quarter fighting in sea battles. In 1704, 1,900 British and 400 Dutch marines prevented Spanish reinforcements reaching their fortress. British ships bombarded the city, while marines and seamen stormed the defences. After three days of naval bombardment and a marine assault, Luttrells' Marines captured the Rock in July 1704. Within a few weeks, Spanish forces began assembling to the north of Gibraltar for an attempt to retake the fortress.

As the Grand Alliance prepared for their assault the priests, women and children, who had taken refuge at the chapel of Europa Point at southern end of the peninsula, began to return to their homes in the town. An English ship fired a warning shot in front of the civilian column, forcing them back out of harm's way, but the shot was mistaken by the rest of the fleet as a signal to resume fire, and the bombardment began again. Under cover of the guns Luttrells landing party did its work.

The foremost sailors clambered into the breached and undefended fort at the New Mole; however, by accident or design the magazine at the fort blew up. Some of the landing party carried lighted gun-matches and, according to Trevelyan, had forgotten the possibility of a powder-magazine. Whatever the cause of the explosion the Alliance suffered between 100–200 casualties. A momentary panic ensued, for the survivors suspected an enemy-laid trap had caused the disaster. There was a rush for the boats, but at this critical moment Captain Whitaker arrived with reinforcements. The landing was supported by a number of Catalan volunteers, after whom Catalan Bay was named. Within a few minutes the attackers had rallied and were proceeding north along the deserted ramparts of the seafront towards Gibraltar. On arriving near Charles V's southern wall of the town, Whitaker halted the sailors and hoisted the Union Flag in a bastion on the shore.

Byng now came ashore with several hundred more seamen. Thus was the town invested by Byng in the south, as well as on its stronger northern side where the marines had landed with Prince George. Meanwhile, the party of women and children stranded at Europa Point had been captured by English sailors. Rooke had given orders that the prisoners were not to be ill-treated, but the desire to recover these women was a further inducement for the defenders to end their resistance. Seeing all was lost, Don Diego agreed to terms that guaranteed the lives and property of those committed to his care. Under the capitulation French subjects were taken prisoner, while any Spaniard who would take an oath of allegiance to 'Charles III' as King of Spain could remain in the town with religion and property guaranteed. However, with the exception of a few families the Spanish elected to depart to the mainland, where shortly afterwards they founded the town of San Roque in sight of their ancient home.

After the twelfth siege, which comprised a six-month bombardment and blockade from the isthmus linking Gibraltar to the mainland, the garrison was no closer to surrendering and the Franco-Spanish army abandoned it, despite the British garrison being heavily outnumbered by 8,000 Spanish and 4,000 French troops. For the part played by Luttrell's Marines in the capture and subsequent defence of the Rock, the battle honour 'Gibraltar, 1704-5' was awarded.

The capture of Gibraltar was recognized as a great achievement in Lisbon and by all the trading interests in the Mediterranean. A month after its capture the Secretary of State, Sir Charles Hedges, described it as 'of great use to us [the English] for securing our trade and interrupting the enemy's'. With the English navy established on the Straits the piratical Moors of the Barbary Coast became reluctant to attack English merchant shipping, and allied themselves with Queen Anne. However, Gibraltar's immediate use as a port was limited, for it could only take a few ships at a time, and ministers did not think they could keep it unless a garrison could be found for its security. John Methuen recommended an English garrison. This was supplied by the marines who had helped take the place, and by several companies of regular troops. Gibraltar was therefore held by English troops and at English cost – but it was in 'Charles III's' name. A year later the Austrian candidate wrote to Queen Anne about 'Ma ville de Gibraltar'. If he had succeeded in his attempt to ascend the throne in Madrid the difficulty of keeping Gibraltar for England would have been politically very great.

The English fleet returned to Tetuan to water. Before fresh orders came from Lisbon there was news of the approach of the French Grand Fleet under Toulouse. In an attempt by the French to retake Gibraltar, the one full-dress naval engagement of the war was fought off Málaga on 24 August; afterwards, French and Spanish troops battered at the land approaches, defended by a small garrison of sailors, soldiers, and marines. These attempts failed, and with the signing of the Treaty of Utrecht in 1713 Britain formally gained control of Gibraltar, which remains a British overseas territory.

Local historic reminders of this period can be found on Queen Anne's statue in Wellington Square. On a pedestal with a canopy the over life-size standing figure of the Queen is in full court dress with regalia, standing on a cuboid marble plinth; the statue is a grade II listed building in the care of English Heritage. It also lists the other great battles fought against the French and Spanish during her reign, including Blenheim, which was led by Churchill, Duke of Marlborough, who was given a palace by a grateful nation in thanks.

This canopied statue of Queen Anne is one of two by the sculptor Bird. The other stands outside St Paul's Cathedral without a canopy. Minehead's statue has faced the square since 1893, before which it stood within the Parish Church. It was presented to the town in 1791 by Sir Jacob Bancks, after whom Bancks Street is named; he was one of Minehead's MPs in the days when the town, with a population of under 2,000, boasted two Members of Parliament.

Sir Jacob Bancks, it should be remembered, married Margaret Luttrell of Dunster Castle after rescuing her from a fire in her house in London. Mrs Luttrell was formerly the heiress Margaret Tregonwell, from Milton Abbas in Dorset. She too, has a road named in her honour in Minehead, Tregonwell Road.

The Napoleonic Wars

The Napoleonic Wars were a series of conflicts involving Napoleon's French Empire and the changing sets of European allies and opposing coalitions that ran from 1803 to 1815. As a continuation of the wars sparked by the French Revolution of 1789, they revolutionized European armies and played out on an unprecedented scale, mainly due to the application of modern mass conscription.

French power rose quickly, conquering most of Europe, but collapsed rapidly after France's disastrous invasion of Russia in 1812. Napoleon's empire ultimately suffered a complete military defeat, resulting in the restoration of the Bourbon monarchy in France. The wars resulted in the dissolution of the Holy Roman Empire. Meanwhile the Spanish Empire began to unravel as the French occupation of Spain weakened Spain's hold over its colonies, providing an opening for nationalist revolutions in Latin America. Col Francis Luttrell played his part in both the Peninsular War and at the Battle of Waterloo. As a direct result of the Napoleonic wars the British Empire became the foremost world power for the next century.

Waterloo was a major battle and the last military engagement of the Napoleonic Wars. It was fought between Napoleon's army and the Seventh Coalition forces, led by the Duke of Wellington, on June 18, 1815, near the Belgian town of Waterloo. The outcome of this fiercely-fought military encounter was a fatal blow inflicted by British forces on Napoleon, marking the end of his Hundred Days Campaign and his ambition to perpetuate himself as an emperor of a Europe-dominated empire.

One of the consequences of the Battle of Waterloo was the emergence of Great Britain as the world's hegemonic power. Having been defeated, Napoleon Bonaparte was exiled to the island of Saint Helena, in the middle of the Atlantic, where he spent the rest of his days until he died in 1821.

The Luttrell family, and indeed the whole of West Somerset, was affected by the French Revolution, even before Napoleon's defeat and exile, as fears were growing that the revolution might spread to England. I 1793 the execution of the French monarch, Louise XVI, and his queen Marie Antoinette, led Britain to become part of a coalition of European nations against France.

There was an ever-present fear of invasion, and the government, in 1798, ordered the formation of a new defence force, the Sea Fencibles. The original Sea Fencibles (a shortened form of defencible), were a naval militia established to provide a close-in line of defence to protect the United Kingdom from invasion by France during the Revolutionary and Napoleonic Wars. Britain's defence rested on two lines: a blockade of French ports provided the first, forward line of defence, and the Sea Fencibles and Martello towers provided the second, coastal, line of defence.

The volunteers were trained in the use of arms and they manned watch and signal towers and fixed and floating batteries along the coasts and ports. They also operated a fleet of gunboats. A member of the Sea Fencibles would spend one day a week training. They were also allowed to choose their own Petty Officers at the rate of one per 25 men. Most importantly, all Sea Fencibles received a certificate that exempted them from impressment into the Navy. The Treasury argued that the exemption from impressment was the principal reason smugglers joined, and there were many of them along this stretch of coast, as impressment was a common punishment for smuggling.

Somerset's force consisted of one captain, four Lieutenants and one hundred and forty four men to protect the whole Somerset coastline from Porlock to Clevedon, with some gun batteries placed at the mouth of the river Avon.

On the last day of December 1803, alarm bells rang and the Lord-Lieutenant of the County and Col of the Somerset Militia issued instructions to all his deputies that formed part of the Home Defence, making it clear that an invasion was imminent:

If an Enemy should land upon our Shore, every possible Exertion should be made immediately to deprive him of the means of sustenance. The Navy will soon cut off his Communications with the sea; the Army will confine him on Shore, in such a Way as to make it impossible for him to draw any supplies. – In this situation he will be forced to lay down his Arms or to give Battle on disadvantageous Terms.

Francis Luttrell was only eleven years old at the time, but he would have witnessed at Dunster Castle all the alarm, hustle, bustle and talk of French invasion from his father John Fownes Luttrell and their near neighbours and cousins, the Wyndham and Trevelyan families. This must certainly have influenced him when he enlisted as an Ensign in the 2nd. Battalion 1st Foot Guards.

In 1805 Napoleon, now Emperor of France, made great preparations for this expected invasion. Admiral Horatio Nelson had just returned from the West Indies to lead the British navy and, in 1805, he won a memorable victory at the Battle of Cape Trafalgar, lying south west off Cadiz near Gibraltar. Nelson's signal to his fleet before the battle of Trafalgar was 'England expects that every man will do his duty' and this decisive encounter stopped Napoleon's forces from advancing to invade Britain. They had been gathered at Boulogne on the English Channel, waiting to cross over in barges. Nelson had known that if he could destroy the French fleet at Trafalgar there would be no invasion.

The wars and politics of Europe had been fairly remote from most people in Somerset till the 1790s. However a former Cistercian monk, Abbe Barbay of Lisieux Abbey, now living in Nether Stowey, gave testimony to the horrors committed by the revolution in France to all who would listen. Also living in Nether Stowey at that time were several young people whose liberal views and behaviour caused great suspicion. The Tory parson of Over Stowey had frequently denounced them. Many thought the midnight walks of the poet Coleridge with William and Dorothy Wordsworth, then staying at Alfoxton, were anything but innocent rambles and that they might have been spying on behalf of Revolutionary France. The 2000 movie *Pandemonium* has this theme as its storyline and graphically displays the friendship and betrayal between two poets living on the Quantocks during the French Revolution.

Fortunately there were others, like Vicar Newton of Old Cleeve and curate of Nether Stowey, and, of course, Tom Poole, who saw them for what they were and by welcoming them made a massive contribution to British national literature.

On 1st March 1815, Napoleon had escaped to France from his exile on the island of Elba. Leaders of the allied powers of Europe, then meeting at the Congress of Vienna, agreed to finally crush France. They began to mass hundreds of thousands of troops on its borders. Napoleon decided to strike before his enemies reached full strength. Quickly he moved 125,000 troops to the Belgian border. A few miles away were 90,000 British, Dutch, Belgians, and Germans under the Duke of Wellington and 115,000 Prussians under Marshal Blücher. Napoleon planned to surprise the two armies, drive between them, and defeat each one separately

Francis Luttrell was actually staying at Dunster Castle when the news arrived of Napoleon's escape from Elba, so he immediately went to London, then to Ramsgate, Ostend, and Ghent, to join his battalion at Enghien. He matriculated at Christ Church, Oxford in 1810, but left without a degree. On 26th December, 1811, at the age of 19, he enlisted as an Ensign in the 2nd. Battalion 1st Foot Guards (later to become the Grenadier Guards) under the command of Lt Colonel Pack.

During the battle of Waterloo he was posted to guard Hougoumont Farm, a strong manor house and known as 'The British Bastion – where the ground was a quagmire piled with dead horses'. Hougoumont Chateau was where most of the bloodiest action was seen.

Hougoumont was a vital anchor and outworks of the allied line. Opposite Col Francis Luttrell's position was the battalion of Jerome Bonaparte, brother of Napoleon. Despite hours of bloody hand-to-hand fighting the small garrison of British Foot held on. It was said that Luttrell had a brief spell of close combat fighting with Jerome Bonaparte himself. His company commander, Lt Col Milnes, and one of the ensigns were killed. By the end of the second day the 2nd Battalion was led by Corporal Thomas Morgan, as all those senior to him had been killed or wounded. This included Francis Luttrell, who had been severely wounded.

He was awarded the General Service Medal with Bars for engagements at Niville and Nive and the Waterloo Medal for Waterloo. Captain Gronow of the Grenadier Guards explains the battle situation:

During the Battle our squares presented a shocking sight. Inside we were nearly suffocated by the smoke and smell from the burnt cartridges. It was impossible to move a yard without treading upon a wounded comrade, or upon the bodies of the dead; and the loud groans of the wounded and dying were most appalling.

At 4 o'clock our square was a perfect hospital, being full of dead, dying and mutilated soldiers. The charges of French Cavalry were in appearance very formidable, but in reality a great relief as there artillery could no longer fire on us.

Another, more detailed, account of the Battle of Waterloo and Hougoumont Farm begins:

The morning and afternoon of the 18th June 1815: At 11am the French bombardment of Hougoumont Farm, on the extreme right of the Allied line, began the battle. The British artillery on the ridge behind the farm replied, cannonading the French infantry massed for the attack on the far side of the valley.

At midday Prince Jerome ordered the assault on Hougoumont and the French infantry columns of his division moved forward to begin the day long struggle around the farm buildings. At about 1.30pm Marshal Ney brought forward 74 French guns over the ridge opposite La Haye Sante followed by the 17,000 infantry of D'Erlon's corps to begin the attack on the Duke of Wellington's centre and left.

After half an hour the barrage stopped, giving way to the

roar of drums as Ney's columns advanced to the attack. The French infantry passed La Haye Sante and marched up to the crest of the ridge, where Picton's 5th division was positioned. As part of the advance a furious assault began on La Haye Sante, held by the King's German Legion, which was to continue intermittently for the rest of the day until the German troops ran out of ammunition and were finally overwhelmed.

As the French infantry approached the hedge at the top of the ridge the line of British infantry stood, fired a volley and charged, driving back the massed French columns.

Cavalry formations were ordered to charge in support of the infantry attack; the Household Brigade (1st and 2nd Life Guards and Royal Horse Guards), the Union Brigade (Royals, Scots Greys and Inniskillings) and Vivian's Hussar Brigade (10th and 18th Hussars and 1st Hussars, King's German Legion).

It is notoriously difficult to pull up cavalry committed to an attack, and the British regiments did not readily respond to the recall orders. In particular the Union Brigade continued to attack across the valley. These regiments charged up to the French gun line on the far ridge, where they were in turn overwhelmed by French cavalry. General Ponsonby, commanding the Union Brigade, was killed. It is of note that of the three regiments in the Union Brigade two, the Greys and Inniskillings, had not served in the Peninsula and lacked battle experience.

At 3pm there was a lull in the battle, the only active fighting being the continuing attack on Hougoument at the western end of the line, which had been sucking in more and more of Reille's corps. The battle began slowly swinging in the Allies' favour as Bl cher's Prussian Army arrived on the field in the South-East.

Napoleon ordered Ney to capture La Haye Sante, considering the farm to be the key to the Allied position. Ney launched this assault with two battalions he found to hand and during the operation formed the view that the Allied army was withdrawing. It is likely that the movements he saw were casualties or prisoners moving to the rear.

Before the French could reach the Allied line the infantry formed squares interlaced with artillery batteries. The French cuirassiers flowed around the squares, but were unable to penetrate them.

During the next three hours some twelve cavalry attacks were made up to the ridge and back. Napoleon, while deprecating the initial attack as premature, felt bound to commit increasing numbers of cavalry to support the assault.

At around 5.30pm Ney launched the final cavalry assault. There were too many regiments, fresh ones mingled with exhausted, and the attack failed yet again. Ney, far too late, launched the sustained infantry assault on La Haye Sante, which was overwhelmed. By now the Prussian assault in the South East on Plancenoit was seriously threatening the French position. Sure that the Allied line was at breaking point, Ney sent desperately to the Emperor for more troops to attack. Napoleon was at this point deploying the Guard to drive the Prussians back from Plancenoit. Once this had been achieved, he resolved to launch the Guard at the main Allied line. By this time Wellington had reorganised his forces and the opportunity that Ney had, this time, correctly identified, had passed.

The Guard marched up to La Haye Sante for the attack. There Napoleon stood aside and left the command to Ney, who led the five battalions up the left hand side of the Brussels road. As they climbed the ridge they came under fire from a curve of batteries assembled to meet them. A deserting French cavalry officer had warned of the Guard's advance.

The Middle Guard threw back the British battalions of Halkett's Brigade, but were assaulted by the Belgian and Dutch troops of General Chassé and Colonel Detmers, who drove them back down the hill.

The 3rd Regiment of Chasseurs approached the ridge opposite Maitland's Brigade of Foot Guards (2nd and 3rd Battalions of the 1st Foot Guards). Wellington called to the brigade commander 'Now Maitland. Now's your time'. One authority had him as saying 'Up Guards, ready'. The Foot Guards stood, fired a volley and charged with the bayonet, driving the French Guard back down the hill.

The last of the French Guard regiments, the 4th Chasseurs, came up in support as the British Guards withdrew back over the ridge.

Sir John Colborne brought the 52nd Foot round to outflank the French column as it passed his brigade, fired a destructive volley into the left flank of the Chasseurs and attacked with the bayonet. The whole of the Guard was driven back down the hill and began a general retreat to the cry of 'La garde recule!'

By the end of the battle the château had been set ablaze by howitzer fire and the buildings were heaped with British casualties. The French were unable to capture Hougoumont, and their own casualties filled the woods and fields and ditches. The two battalions that defended Hougoumont suffered 500 dead and wounded out of strengths of 2,000.

Some years later an English clergyman bequeathed £500 to be given to the bravest Briton from the battle. The selection was referred to the Duke of Wellington, who nominated Lieutenant Colonel McDonnell of the Coldstream Guards for his defence of Hougoumont. Colonel McDonnell gave half the sum to Sergeant Graham.

McDonnell and Graham had held the gates of a farmhouse which the Coldstream Guards were defending from the French. The actions carried out on that date are a little obscure, but what is known is that the Duke of Wellington later stated that Hougoumont Farm was key in the Battle of Waterloo, and that if it had been lost Wellington's flank would have been turned and the outcome of the battle might have been very different.

The Coldstream Guards celebrate the defence of Hougoumont every year with the ceremony of the hanging of the brick.

The Muster Roll for Lt./Col. Milne's Company for

Waterloo reveals the extent of the casualties suffered. The company consisted of 100 men, of which there were four officers, five sergeants, five corporals, three drummers and 84 troopers. Of these 10 were killed or died of their wounds and 29 more were wounded, many severely. The officers, sergeants and corporals seem to have suffered extremely badly. Out of four officers two were killed. A Thomas Brown had been killed two days previously at Quatre Bras and Francis Luttrell had been severely wounded. Of the five sergeants, four were wounded. Of the five corporals, one was killed and three wounded. Of the 84 troopers seven were killed and 28 wounded. The drummers suffered no casualties. Despite hours of bloody hand-to-hand combat with the garrison of British Foot soldiers, it never fell.

The corporal who was killed, George Dickins, had been appointed only the previous day. Corporal Thomas Morgan, despite bayonet wounds to the lip and tongue and musket wounds to his knee and neck, took command at Hougoumont during the final charge, as all company officers and non-commissioned officers were either dead or wounded. He received a medal and gratuity for meritorious conduct and was discharged with a pension in 1833.

About 10,000 men fell in and around Hougoumont, the overwhelming majority of them French. Wellington used about 3500 men in all to hold the farm. The daily ration at the château for the soldiers amounted to 1½ lb (0.7kg) bread or 1lb (0.5kg) biscuit, 1lb (0.5kg) beef or mutton and half a pint (0.5 kg) wine or a third of a pint (0.3 litres) rum, although they often found themselves on half-rations or no rations at all (p. 61 *War Walks*, by Richard Holmes).

Francis Luttrell was awarded the General Service Medal, with bars for Nivelle and Nive and the Waterloo Medal for Waterloo. He died on the 4th of January 1862 and was buried at Dunster, where there is a stained glass window in memory of him and his wife, Emma Louise Drewe, who survived until 1881. They had nine children.

The *West Somerset Free Press* of January 11th 1862 had this to say regarding his death:

DEATH OF COL FRANCIS LUTTRELL

We regret to record the death of Lieut-Colonel Francis Fownes Luttrell, of Kilve Court, in this county, who expired at his residence on Saturday last, at the advanced age of seventy. Lieut-Col Luttrell served with the Grenadier Guards in the Peninsula, and has received the war medal with two clasps for the battles of Niville and Nive. He served also the campaign of 1815, and was present at the battle of Waterloo. He was for some years Lieut-Colonel of the Second Somerset Militia, and was a magistrate and deputy lieutenant for his county. His remains will be deposited in the family vault at Dunster church on Saturday (this day).

On the following Saturday, 18th January, this more detailed report appeared:

The Late Colonel Luttrell: A contemporary of this week publishes the following memoir:

'*While our sorrow is still alive to the loss of the Prince*

Consort, our own immediate neighbourhood has to lament the loss of one of its most distinguished characters by the recent death of the above named gentleman. In a locality like this, where public men of business are so scarce, he was deservedly considered and used as public property, and was on all occasions – and numerous indeed they were – looked up for counsel and advice. Unpretending to deep research and learning, he possessed an understanding and judgement so truly correct that it carried with it the accordance of those whose pretensions would have overborne weaker minds. When he made up his mind, after mature consideration on both sides of a question, his decisions generally obtained the concurrence of his colleagues, and were seldom repudiated or complained of, even by the losing party. The neighbourhood, and we may say the whole Western division of the County, is deeply indebted to him for the active discharge of most of its public business in his capacities as Chairman of the Quarter Sessions and Williton Board of Guardians (from the commencement of the Union to the day of his death), as Magistrate, Commissioner of Taxes and Turnpike, as a ready and kind arbitrator to reconcile differences without expense between man and his neighbour; and in all these complicated duties his opinion and decisions were always received as a safe basis to act upon and as the results of a honest, straight forward and enlightened mind. Although he never assumed superiority and distinction, it was always conceded to him as his due; and well was it bestowed upon one possessing such strong natural abilities, and such a high sense of honour and honesty to carry them out. Besides these public qualifications, his apparently retiring manners may have

concealed from public gaze his really kind and social instincts;
but he had a tear for distress, and a mite for the needy; he had
a heart to feel and a ready hand to save, as well as a manly
courage and fortitude that braved the dangers of Waterloo. In
the earlier part of his life he served his country for fifteen years
as an officer in the Grenadier Guards, two of which were spent
in the Peninsular War; he was in the whole of the Waterloo
Campaign, and was engaged in that ever memorable battle on
the 18th. June 1815 and was wounded in that dreadful struggle
in the orchard at Huguenot, since which he was made
Lieutenant- Colonel in the 2nd. Somerset Militia, form the
active service of which he retired on the 4th June, 1859 ; but
on account of his long service her majesty allowed him to retain
his rank. It is somewhat singular that on the day of his death
he had numbered 32 years as Master of the West Somerset Fox-
Hounds; and it must be conceded by all who witnessed his
gentlemanly demeanour and his thorough judgement in the
field, that he fully deserved the mark of regret and respect which
all classes are unfeignedly paying to his memory.'

There is a portrait of him in the library and also at the
Somerset Military Museum in Taunton. The Dunster
Castle portrait has inscribed on the back 'Painted and
presented by Ensign W. Barrett on 26th February 1855'.

In the Somerset Military Museum there is also a
portrait of him in the uniform of the 2nd. Somerset
Militia, probably painted in the 1840's. Interestingly he
appears to have both his eyes, so he obviously did not lose
one at Waterloo. David Eliot, the curator provided the
following information: The portrait is a tinted painted

photograph by W. Waterhouse, 36 Abingdon Villas, Kensington, June 1865. David Eliot suggests that the portrait is circa 1862 and shows Lt. Francis Luttrell in the uniform of the 2nd. Somerset Militia, circa 1862.) If this is correct the portrait was done a short time before his death. His Waterloo and Peninsular Medals are also lodged at the Museum.

It is also worth mentioning here other connections with the name Luttrell and maritime adventures and warfare who were sailed the seven seas.

A familiar name descended from Nicholas Luttrell of Dunster Castle is Dr Edward Luttrell, forefather of Australian Luttrells. In 1807, as the Napoleonic Wars were reaching a climax on the other side of the world, Dr Edward Luttrell was on board the HMS *Porpoise* serving as ship's surgeon, having left the shores of England in 1804 with a view to settling in Australia with his wife and seven children. Captain Cook had previously sailed these waters and had already discovered Australia some thirty years before in 1770.

Whilst serving on board the *Porpoise* in New South Wales, Edward Luttrell was given permission to go inland to visit his family in Paramatta, where he fell ill and was unable to return to his ship when summoned to do so by his captain. Smitten by fever, he wrote an explanation to his captain. This was the irascible Commodore Bligh of Mutiny on the Bounty fame, who refused to believe him and ordered him to come on board dead or alive and put a dishonourable 'R' against his name in the ship's log, meaning 'runner'. It took ten years for the insult to be removed by the Board of Admiralty.

However, we find that in 1816 Luttrell was a member of the exclusive Waterloo Club founded by Colonel Davey in Van Diemen's Land after the defeat of Napoleon and France. Members of the club were considered to be the top echelon of Hobart society and were attended at functions by convicts. Dying on 10th June 1824, he was buried in Hobart, Tasmania, founded in 1804 as a penal colony.

Edward's sons were also seafarers and all met untimely ends, with Hungerford Luttrell, the eldest, also a surgeon, dying of fever off the coast of Africa. Edward, the second eldest, was lost at sea in the Indian Ocean on board the *Governor Macquarie*, in 1811. Robert, the third son, was killed by native Aborigine peoples at Paramatta in New South Wales in 1812 and Oscar Luttrell, the youngest, was also killed by Aborigines near Melbourne in 1838.

Returning to the Battle of Trafalgar. Two ships at the battle, HMS Mars and HMS Achilles were named after ships previously commanded by a Luttrell. Captain John Olmius Luttrell, 3rd Earl of Carhampton (11 December 1739–19 March 1829), styled The Honourable John Luttrell between 1768 and 1787 and as The Honourable John Olmius Luttrell between 1787 and 1829, was an Irish naval commander and politician who joined the Navy as Lieutenant on 10th October 1758. From 5th August 1762 to 25th October 1763 he captained the *Mars*, a ship of 74 guns (in service from 1759-1784), in which he probably proceeded to North America before the conclusion of the war. From 24th May 1765 to 3rd June 1768 he captained HMS *Achilles*, a guardship of 60 guns, in service from 1757-1784 and stationed at Portsmouth.

George Duff commanded the *Mars* and Richard King the *Achilles* at Cape Trafalgar. Captain Duff was killed in action and was buried at sea off Cape Trafalgar. His monument can be seen in the crypt of St Pauls Cathedral, London.

At Dunster Castle there is a two-masted model sailing ship which belonged to the late Sir Walter Luttrell, described simply as 'black painted wooden model of a boat, rigged with no sail'. It was restored by his uncle, Vice Admiral Collingwood, in the 1920s.

The sailing ship HMS *Collingwood* gained its name from Lord Collingwood, a distinguished Admiral in the 19th century. He was a colleague of Nelson and took command of the British Fleet at Trafalgar after Nelson was mortally wounded. He died at sea off Minorca and was buried next to Nelson in St Paul's Cathedral.

There have been three ships in the Navy named Collingwood. John Alexander Fownes Luttrell served on the first, which was launched at Pembroke in 1841. The ship, an 80-gun wooden man o' war, weighed 2,585 tons, was 190 feet in length and had a crew of 750. Her armament comprised four 68-pounder, sixty-eight 32-pounders and four 18-pounder guns, together with four 32-pounder cannonades. She was one of the last wooden battleships built. The last Collingwood was sold for breaking up in December 1922 and the name remains today with the Royal Navy training base at HMS Collingwood, Plymouth. —— PORTSMOUTH

John Alexander Fownes Luttrell (Captain, d 1889), second son of Alexander Fownes Luttrell of Edington near Bridgwater, also had a naval career. He entered the Navy in October 1846 as Admiralty Midshipman on the *Collingwood*. He eventually became a Post Captain and then a commander in the Coastguard. From the Admiralty, Royal Marines, on October 22nd 1873 a statement was issued:

In accordance with the provisions of the Order of Council, the undermentioned commander has been placed on the Retired List of their rank 1st Instance.

Commander: John Alexander Fownes Luttrell.

We also know of the mariner James Luttrell (1751 - 1788), MP for Stockbridge & Dover and son of the 1st Earl of Carhampton and Surveyor-General of the Ordinance, 1784-8. He was praised by King George III for his bravery. James Luttrell was descended from the Luttrells of Luttrelltown near Dublin, the son of Simon and Judith (Maria Lawes) Luttrell and brother of John, Simon, Henry Lawes and Temple. He was made Captain in the Royal Navy in 1781 and served possibly from 1770–1778. He took part in the American War of Independence and commanded the *Mediator* in action with the American and French Fleet in 1782.

On 16 March 1782 he was appointed to the *Mediator* of 44 guns. In December, while waiting off Ferrol to intercept an American frigate lying there, he fell in with a squadron of five of the enemy's vessels, storeships or privateers, which were heavily armed and with an aggregate of over six hundred men. As the *Mediator* stood towards them they formed into line of battle, and presented a formidable appearance, but Luttrell bore down on them, and after a few broadsides cut off one of the largest, the *Alexandre*, and compelled her to strike.

While he was taking possession of her, the others scattered and fled. It was not till five hours later that the *Mediator* came up with another of the vessels, the *Ménagère*, which she captured after a running fight of nearly three hours more. The next day two of the others were in sight, partially dismasted, but Luttrell felt unequal to any further attack.

The following day a desperate but unsuccessful attempt was made by his prisoner to set fire to the *Mediator*, but the prizes were brought safely to England. In April 1783 Luttrell was moved into the *Ganges* of 74 guns, and the following September he was appointed Surveyor-General of the Ordnance, a post which he held till his death, from consumption, on 23 December 1788. In 1775 he was returned to parliament by the borough of Stockbridge in Hampshire, which he represented till 1784, when he was returned by Dover.

The King, George III, wrote to the 1st Lord of the Admiralty, Keppel, the following year in praise of James Luttrell, saying 'The skill as well as bravery shown by Captain Luttrell deserves much appreciation'. On his death bed King George III is said to have remembered Luttrell as 'the best of that strange family'.

CHAPTER SIXTEEN

World War II

Surprisingly, during the previous World War, no male member of the family was actually in residence at Dunster Castle, though there was Mary Luttrell at Dunster, whose service to the Red Cross was well known. However during at least two periods in the castle's history it has been left deserted and at one time it was left derelict, 'a sad picture of departed greatness' as one visitor wrote in 1845. There was, I believe, a retainer to look after the essentials of the property. When George Luttrell died in 1910 at the ripe age of eighty four years, his son, Alexander, decided against moving into the castle and remained at the family's historic home at Court House, East Quantoxhead.

In 1914, before the outbreak of World War I, Alexander Luttrell's son, Geoffrey returned to Australia to become, at the age of 27, private secretary to the Governor General of Australia, Sir Ronald Munro Ferguson, his uncle on his mother's side. When World War I broke out, despite several attempts to enlist, he was turned down for military service on health grounds. Told he should lead an outdoor life rather than work in an office, he worked for a year as a professional fisherman in partnership with an old fisherman, off the coast of Victoria in south-east Australia, living on what he earned. During this time he met Alys Anne Wilson Bridges, an Australian whose father had been a rear admiral. They married in Australia in 1918. The following year their first son, Walter, was born. The family returned to Somerset in 1920 and took up residence at Dunster Castle, which had been empty since the death of his grandfather George in 1910.

A certain Richard Luttrell served in the war, and there is a memorial plaque with his name on at the memorial hall in the village, but eleven other brave soldiers did not return.

World War Two was the largest armed conflict in history and the bloodiest, deadliest war the world had ever seen. More than 38 million people died, many of them innocent civilians. It was also the most destructive war in history. Fighting raged in many parts of the world and more than 50 nations took part in the war, which changed the world forever by the introduction of new and powerful weapons, culminating in the first use of nuclear weapons.

In 1940, after the evacuation of the British Army from Dunkirk, there was a serious threat of invasion by the Germans. Preparations were made throughout the country to resist any attempts at landings, by sea or air, of enemy forces. A national scheme of local defence volunteers was established. This force later became the Home Guard and was gradually trained and equipped with weapons of all types. The coastline of England, including that of Somerset, was protected by barbed wire defences, concrete 'pill-boxes' and obstructions on the beaches to prevent landings by gliders or shallow-draught barges. A 'stop' line was constructed from Highbridge in Somerset to Seaton in Devon, following rivers, canals and the railway lines. Obstacles to prevent enemy movement in the event of a successful landing were constructed, and bridges and towns were protected by 'tank-traps' of concrete and steel girders. The remains of some of these strongpoints still remind us of the last unfulfilled threat of invasion, during the Second World War and it was in this year the first bombs fell just outside Taunton.

Walter Luttrell enlisted as a trooper in 1939 at the outbreak of the war and was subsequently commissioned into the 15th/19th The King's Royal Hussars with their famous motto 'Merebimur' ('we shall be worthy'). The King's Royal Hussars was a cavalry regiment of the British Army, created as part of the reduction in cavalry in the aftermath of the First World War. It was formed by the amalgamation of the 15th The King's Hussars and the 19th Royal Hussars (Queen Alexandra's Own) on 11 April 1922, becoming the 15th/19th Hussars. It briefly dropped the '19th' from its title in 1932, becoming the 15th The King's Royal Hussars, before regaining it the following year.

In 1992 Walter's regiment was amalgamated with the 13/18 Royal Hussars (Queen Mary's Own) to become the

Light Dragoons. Both regiments date back to the 1700s and were originally known as Light Dragoons. As the name suggests, Light Dragoons were light cavalry mounted on fast horses, able to move quickly across the battlefield.

At the outbreak of the Second World War the regiment was part of the 3rd Infantry Division, based in York, serving as the divisional reconnaissance regiment (3 September 1939 - 30 March 1940). The regiment was deployed with the division as part of the British Expeditionary Force, and fought in the Battle of France. During this time, the regiment was transferred to the 2nd Armoured Reconnaissance Brigade (30 March 1940 - 22 June 1940). The regiment was decimated during the German advance, and was evacuated from Dunkirk during Operation Dynamo. In the evacuation all the regiment's remaining armour and vehicles were left behind.

Sir Walter Luttrell is listed among the most notable soldiers in the history of the regiment, alongside names such as Captain Louis Nolan (1818–1854), who was a British Army officer, an authority on cavalry tactics, and best known for his controversial role in launching the disastrous Charge of the Light Brigade during the famous Battle of Balaclava in 1854. He was also the first casualty of 15th Hussars during that engagement of the Crimean War. Although the British eventually won the battle, confusion amongst their officers resulted in 250 of the 673 men in the Light Brigade being killed or wounded during the reckless charge.

Three episodes in the battle, the Charge of the Heavy Brigade, the Thin Red Line and the Charge of the Light Brigade, are such icons of courage and achievement for the British Army that it is not surprising the military authorities awarded Balaclava as a battle honour to the regiments involved.

A Bridge Too Far, the 1977 epic war film, tells the story of the failure of Operation Market Garden during World War II, the Allied attempt to break through German lines and seize several bridges in the occupied Netherlands, including one at Arnhem, with the main objective of outflanking German defences. The name of the film comes from an unconfirmed comment attributed to British Lieutenant-General Frederick Browning, deputy commander of the First Allied Airborne Army, who told Field Marshal Bernard Montgomery, the operation's architect, before the operation: 'I think we may be going a bridge too far'.

Major Blackwood of the 4th Parachute Brigade summed up the situation on 19 September: 'Message to say that our attack on the Arnhem bridge had been beaten back and that German tanks had outflanked and surrounded us... Our orders were brief – wait for the tanks, give them everything we had in the way of grenades, shoot up as many infantry as we could before we died.'

Operation Market Garden (17–25 September 1944) was an unsuccessful Allied military operation, fought in the Netherlands and Germany in the Second World War. It was the largest airborne operation up to that time. Field

Marshal Montgomery's goal was to force an entry into Germany and over the Rhine. He wanted to circumvent the northern end of the Siegfried Line, and this required an operation to seize the bridges across the Maas (Meuse) river and two arms of the Rhine (the Waal and the Lower Rhine) as well as several smaller canals and tributaries. Crossing the Lower Rhine would allow the Allies to encircle Germany's industrial heartland in the Ruhr from the north. It made large-scale use of airborne forces, whose tactical objectives were to secure the bridges and allow a rapid advance by armoured units into Northern Germany.

The 11th Armoured Division, minus Sir Walter Luttrell's regiment, the 15th/19th King's Royal Hussars, who were supporting XXX Corps, commenced its advance across the Escaut Canal at Lille-St-Hubert. It had orders to clear the enemy forces east of Eindhoven and Grave, but through delays they were too late to offer any immediate protection to the airborne corridor. On Sunday 17 September, 500 gliders and 1,500 aircraft flew over the men of XXX Corps, whose job was to follow beneath them in their tanks and trucks supported by Luttrell's Kings Royal Hussars. As the aircraft flew over, the Allied guns began a huge barrage to hit the Germans guarding the road ahead. The weather that day was beautiful, with a cloudless blue sky and a warming autumn sun.

The 11th Armoured Division set the benchmark for all British armoured divisions in northwest Europe. All companies from the Division use all the British special rules found in the 'Flames of War' rulebook Throughout the autumn, the 11th Armoured Division and the 101st Airborne worked closely together on many occasions. In fact, for one week during Market Garden Operation, Luttrells 15th/19th Hussars were detached to the American paratroopers and served directly under their command. In the Ardennes, the 29 Armoured Brigade made contact with a 101st Reinforcement group shoring up the defences at key bridge crossings, sealing off the major population centres of Brussels and Antwerp from the German offensive.

Montgomery issued his directive on 14 September 1944. The ground phase of the campaign- coded GARDEN - had two major objectives: first, a rapid advance from the British Second Army's bridgehead across the Meuse-Escaut Canal northward to the Rhine and the Zuider Zee, thus flanking the Siegfried Line; second, possession of the area between Arnhem and the Zuider Zee, preparatory to an advance across the Ijssel River on to the North German Plain. The initial advance was to be along a very narrow front in the direction of Eindhoven, Veghel, Grave, Nijmegen, Arnhem, and Apeldoorn.

In the words of Montgomery, the drive was to be rapid and violent, one made without regard for what was happening on the flanks. The task fell chiefly to the Guards Armoured Division and to the 43 and 50 Infantry Divisions. To facilitate and expedite their advance, General Brereton's newly-organized command undertook the largest airborne operation yet attempted.

The operation had as its purpose the laying of airborne troops across the waterways on the general axis of advance and the capture of vital road, rail, and pontoon bridges between Eindhoven and Arnhem. It was in this operation that Sir Walter Luttrell first engaged the enemy. In September 1944 Luttrell, then a captain, was in the bridgehead over the Meuse-Escaut Canal when a troop of his squadron came under fire in difficult, thickly-wooded country. Luttrell was ordered to extricate the troop; the troop leader was one of many casualties and two of the tanks had broken tracks. Despite being attacked from all sides, he got the tracks repaired, withdrew the troops and inflicted heavy losses on the enemy.

In April 1945 Luttrell's squadron seized the pass up the Teutoberger Wald, south of Osnabruck, and fought for a whole day along the top of this feature, entirely unsupported and against powerful and determined opposition. The bold and accurate use of his 95 mm guns took a severe toll of the enemy, and the citation for his MC paid tribute to his calm leadership, skill and magnificent courage in the most testing situations.

The major units within the 11th Armoured Division were the Royal Armoured Corps, comprising the 3rd Battalion Royal Tank Regiment, 2nd Fife and Forfar Yeomanry, 15/19 Kings Royal Hussars and the Inns of Court. The Infantry units within the 159 Infantry Brigade were the 1st Battalion The Herefordshire Regiment, the 3rd Monmouthshire Regiment, the 4th Battalion Kings Shropshire Light Infantry and later the Cheshire Regiment. All these were additionally supported by Signals, Engineers and Sapper units and the complete

Division bore the insignia of The Black Bull (a black charging bull with red hooves set upon a yellow background) with great pride.

It is possibly because of the speed of the advance of the Allied armies through Germany in the next few days, stopping only for short periods at the many river crossings and particularly upon the discovery of the concentration camp at Belsen, that this battle at the Teutoburger Wald was so poorly recorded. The loss of so many 3rd Monmouth Officers during these fateful days and the lack of 'O' group reports did little to record the heroism of the men of the 3rd Monmouths and the 1st Herefords who had been in action during those few early days of April. The award of the Victoria Cross and the Military Cross and Military Medals to officers and other ranks of the 1st Herefords indicates this, as at a local level, Luttrell's award for bravery testifies.

The casualties to the Allied forces over these few early days of April 1945 were numerous, particularly to officers and men of the 3rd Mons, the 1st Herefords and the 4th KOSB. The support units of the 159 Infantry Brigade and the 11th Armoured Division also suffered to a lesser degree during the Luftwaffe air attacks.

Having suffered so many casualties, killed or wounded, the 3rd Monmouths, who had been with the 11th Armoured since its arrival in France, had ceased to be a front line fighting unit and were replaced by the Cheshire Regiment.

While all this activity was taking place, on the 1st and 2nd April, the armoured units of Captain Walter Luttrell's regiment, the 15/19 Hussars, had travelled eastward towards Brockterbeck and Tecklenburg along the southern edge of the forest and then proceeded to traverse the second road which led over and through the forest towards Ibbenburen. This road wound uphill through a tree-lined gorge, a difficult route, particularly without infantry support. The speed of the new Comet tank and the dash and verve of the tank crews took this attack to the north side of the forest, whereupon it turned east across open farmland towards the Ibbenburen/Munster road, where the 1st Herefords had attacked. Firing all the way along the forest edge and inflicting many casualties, they eventually called the attack off due to the poor light and boggy ground, several tanks being bogged down, although they were recovered later. After retiring to their original start point at Brockterbeck, the attack then turned towards Tecklenburg.

While the fighting was ongoing in the Teutoburger Wald, Onasbruck was captured by the British and Canadians of 8th Corps on the 4th April. Having crossed the Dortmund Ems canal relatively easy, Onasbruck was soon cleared. Heavy resistance was met on the outskirts of Minden. The bridges had been blown, but when the 6th Airborne Division entered in the evening the town was empty and Minden fell on the 5th April 1945.

Minden was actually an objective of the US 9th Army, who arrived soon afterwards. They had captured Munster on the 3rd April and they took Hameln on the 7th. On the 8th the Canadians took Wunsdorf. Bergen-Belsen was liberated by the 11th Armoured Division on the 15th April. By this time the British 2nd Army was moving swiftly towards the Baltic, and although they met some heavy resistance in some places it was soon repelled.

Towards the end of April the Germans were surrendering more readily, as they were well aware of the advancing Russians in the east and certainly did not want to fall into their hands. Some German soldiers were actually surrendering with their wives and children, as they were terrified of being taken prisoner by the Russians.

After the war Sir Walter Luttrell accompanied 15/19 KRH to Palestine before retiring from the Army in 1946. He farmed near Tiverton, Devon, for four years and then moved into the family's ancestral home at East Quantoxhead in 1952.

Just after the war Geoffrey Luttrell, father of Sir Walter, made a series of broadcasts to Canada on the history of the castle and the surrounding area. His transatlantic connection mirrored the interest and care he and Alys had shown to the wounded American officers during World War II; they were invited to convalesce in the castle. In gratitude the American naval personnel donated a large gas cooker for use in the castle kitchen, to supplement the Victorian cooking range which can still be seen to this day.

Like her husband Geoffrey, Alys was actively involved in public service during the war, particularly from 1944, when Geoffrey became squire, until his death in 1957. For more than 30 years she was associated with the St John Ambulance movement; she was an honorary Vice

President of the Minehead division of the St John Ambulance Brigade. In World War II she was a Vice President of the County St John Nursing Division and in 1944 she became County President of the Order of St John. In 1954 she was appointed Dame of the Venerable Order of the Hospital of St John of Jerusalem.

From 1943 to 1944 she made the castle available as a convalescent home for Naval and American Officers. She ran it like a big house party, and for some time the castle was full up with 12 officers and staff, continually changing as men recovered and others arrived. She was also a member of the Exmoor Forces Welfare Committee. Alys was involved in many and varied causes for the general war effort. For instance she inaugurated West Somerset's Bomber and Fighter plane collections, and was President of the committee for Minehead District of the Penny-a-Week and Rural Pennies Fund of the Red Cross, which raised over £7,500 from 1939 to 1945.

After World War II she became a member of the Management Committee of Broadlands Retirement Home, giving the residents a TV set in 1953 so that they could watch the Coronation of Elizabeth II.

One of her staff describes Alys as 'a very distinguished looking lady; tall erect, with an aristocratic face. She had a very strong personality and could be somewhat formidable until one had time to get to know her. Alys loved flowers and took pride in the garden.'

A letter by Alys, sent to a Miss Val Piper Smith, after Alys was house-bound reads: 'I am happy when people feel the, to me, lovely atmosphere of my home which seems to have stood for courage and steadfastness and peaceful serenity (despite its warring history) all these many centuries. What a charming gift you sent me – nothing could have given me greater delight especially as I had to 'stay put' in my room with laryngitis and the sight of the lovely flowers meant a lot to me.'

Val had known Alys Luttrell and her family, and become almost part of it, since the 1940s when she came to Dunster as an evacuee during the war. She well remembered Geoffrey Luttrell frequently sitting in a large sofa in the mid 1950s in the 'Squire's Room', watching cricket on television during the summer months. When Sir Walter Luttrell gave the castle and thirty acres of old deer park to the National Trust in 1976, Val was one of the first to volunteer at the property and remained a volunteer for almost thirty-five years till her death in 2011.

Geoffrey Luttrell's wife was Alys Ann Wilson Bridges, daughter of Rear-Admiral Walter Bogue Bridges. Sir Walter Luttrell's wife, Hermione, who is also now deceased, was the eldest daughter of Captain Cecil Bernard Gunston and Lady Doris Gwendoline Hamilton-Temple-Blackwood, eldest daughter of the second Marquess of Dufferin and Ava. Her father, who died when she was eleven, was on the Stock Exchange and they lived initially north of the Park in Southwark Crescent. After her father's death the family moved to Canning Place, London.

In his memoirs, Sir Walter remarks: My unit trained for various armoured roles including amphibious tanks and were on standby for going to the Middle East, but we were never sent there. During a spell of training in Northumberland in 1942, I came down to London for a long weekend's leave and met Hermione Gunston for the first time on the Friday evening. We got engaged before I returned to my Regiment on the following Tuesday.'

Hermione was nineteen at the time of her marriage and about to join the Wrens (WRNS), but felt that service life would not be compatible with newly-married life, especially with a husband on the move, and changed her mind. During the first year of the marriage they managed to live in various cottages near to Sir Walter's postings. When this was no longer possible, she joined the SOE in Baker Street.

From a flat in Sloane Street, Hermione Luttrell worked for SOE until the end of the War, through V1s, V2s and an era of shortages.

On August 6, 1945 at 8.15 am, the uranium atom bomb exploded 580 metres above the city of Hiroshima with a blinding flash, creating a giant fireball and sending surface temperatures to 4,000°C. Fierce heat and radiation burst out in every direction, unleashing a high-pressure shockwave. It vaporised tens of thousands of people and animals, melted buildings and streetcars and reduced a 400-year-old city to dust. World War II came to an end.

As a consequence of the war, the Allies created the United Nations, a new global organization for international cooperation and diplomacy. The UN agreed to outlaw wars of aggression in an attempt to avoid a third world war. The devastated great powers of Western Europe formed the European Coal and Steel Community (which later evolved into the European Union) in an attempt to avoid another war by economic cooperation and a common market for important natural resources.

This war marked the end of almost one thousand years of conflict for the two families who occupied the castle during this period. Both families, the Mohuns and the Luttrells, have descendants across the world who make frequent visits to Dunster Castle, which is always at the top of their 'must see' list on arrival in the UK.

It has been almost 70 years since the end of World War Two and although this war was the last for Dunster Castle's families the Luttrell military legacy lives on to this day in the form of The Yorkshire Regiment (14th/15th, 19th and 33rd/76th Foot) with the 19th Foot origins at Dunster Castle, which is considered by the Green Howards to be their spiritual home.

A tribute to the Green Howards

The Green Howards Regiment can trace its history back to the 17th Century and Dunster Castle in Somerset. They were originally known as Luttrell's Foot, then at a later period the Nineteenth Foot. The Regimental Headquarters is now in Richmond, Yorkshire, but to this day they uphold that Dunster Castle is their historic and spiritual home.

The regiment is perhaps better known as the "Green Howards". This title dates back to the wars of Austrian Succession in the mid 1700s, when the Colonel was the Hon Charles Howard (at this time, regiments were often referred to by the name of their Colonel). As the regiment was brigaded with another whose name was also Howard, there was duplication, so this regiment, which wore green facings to its uniform, became the "Green" Howards and the other the "Buff" Howards. The "Green Howards" and the "Buffs" were names still in use in 1914-1918. The nickname "Green Howards" stuck, and survived until 1920 when it became the official title of the regiment.

The Green Howards (Alexandra, Princess of Wales's Own Yorkshire Regiment), frequently known as the Yorkshire Regiment until the 1920s, was an infantry regiment of the British Army, in the King's Division. It served under various titles until it was amalgamated with The Prince of Wales' Own Regiment of Yorkshire and The Duke of Wellington's Regiment, all Yorkshire-based regiments in the King's Division to form The Yorkshire Regiment on 6 June 2006.

The regiment was first raised on 19th November 1688 by Colonel Francis Luttrell at Dunster Castle in Somerset, for service under William, Prince of Orange when he commissioned Francis Luttrell at Exeter 1688. In the following year household accounts shows the bill for uniform and other officer's attire, bought in London, were expensive indeed and, as befitted the age, flamboyant.

In January 1689 he had a coat of "fine Segovia serge" a coat of "fine blue cloth," lined with "black rasdejane," a "black ratteene waistcoat" and breeches of "black flowered velvet." The buttons were of "black silk". A waistcoat of white and gold silk costing "£17 2s 3d" in April of that year, the material alone costing 55s per yard. In that month there were extra charges on Col Luttrell's uniform apparently supplied by Parliament "to pay for the lining of your embroidered coat, being of richer satin and much better than the lineing of the other officers £1 6s. To pay for blew cloth for your coat, being much better than the other officers, 10s.[1]"

Of course Col Luttrell was responsible for the liveries of the men in his service, with blue, black and gold the dominant colours of the Luttrells' historic badge and crest. This is reflected today in the footman's uniform worn during Victorian servants' tours of Dunster Castle.

When the regiment was put on a regular basis the following February, 1689, Col Luttrell's brother Alexander received a commission in it as Captain. After the death of Colonel Francis Luttrell in 1690 there was a dispute with his successor, Thomas Erle, Alexander Luttrell, who along with several other officers resigned in disgust at the appointment. Alexander went on to glory in Luttrell's Marines at the capture of Gibraltar for the UK in 1704.

The 12th July 1690 was the day of the decisive victory at the Battle of the Boyne and saw the Regiment's support for Prince William against King James I and its first active service in what became known as the Glorious Revolution, as the Prince assumed the title of King William of Orange. This victory is celebrated to this day in Northern Ireland.

The regiment first became associated with, and affiliated to, the North Riding of Yorkshire in 1782 when it was granted the title of "the 19th (First Yorkshire North Riding Regiment) of Foot". The title was given when the regiment returned from taking part in the American War of Independence. The regiment was not actually based in

[1] Lyte: History of Dunster

the county until much later. It was only in 1873 that Richmond in Yorkshire became the regiment's home town.

In 1875 the late Queen Alexandra, then Princess of Wales and formerly a Princess of the Royal House of Denmark, presented the regiment with new Colours to replace those which had been carried throughout the Crimean War. The regiment was then graciously granted the title of "The Princess of Wales's Own".

In 1881, on the introduction of the territorial system, the name of the regiment was again altered to become "The Princess of Wales's Own Yorkshire Regiment". Following the South African War, the word "Alexandra" was added.

Finally, in 1920 the title of the Regiment became "The Green Howards (Alexandra, Princess of Wales's Own Yorkshire Regiment)".

During the First World War (1914-1918) 24 battalions of the Regiment were raised, and the Regiment took part in most of the principal battles and campaigns of the war, including that in North Russia in 1919.

Over 65,000 men served in the ranks of the Regiment, and of these over 7,500 were killed and nearly 24,000 wounded. Twelve Victoria Crosses were awarded during World War I.

Between 1918 and 1939, the Regiment took part in the third Afghan War of 1919, the operations in Palestine during 1938, the Waziristan operations of 1937-1939, and many other internal security duties overseas including those in Shanghai between 1927 and 1930.

In the Second World War (1939-1945), twelve battalions of the Regiment were raised. The Regiment fought in Norway, the Western Desert, Sicily, Italy, Burma, France, Holland and Germany. Two battalions were amongst the first to land in the assault on D-Day 1944, where a member of the 6th Battalion was the only Victoria Cross to be awarded on D-Day.

Between 1949 and 1952 the Regiment served with great distinction in the campaign against the Chinese and Malayan Communist Terrorists in Malaya. In the years since 1952, the Regiment has served in Afghanistan, Austria, West Germany, Suez, Cyprus, Hong Kong, Libya, Belize, Berlin and England. It has distinguished itself in operations in Northern Ireland. One Regimental Officer was killed in action while serving with very great gallantry in the Falkland Islands in 1982. Elements of the First Battalion took part in the Gulf War in 1991, and in operations in Bosnia 1996-97.

In 2004, as part of the reorganisation of the infantry, it was announced that the Green Howards would merge with the Prince of Wales' Own Regiment of Yorkshire (PWO) and the Duke of Wellington's Regiment (DWR) to form the new Yorkshire Regiment. The official rebadging took place on 6 June 2006, while elements of the regiment were stationed in Bosnia and Kosovo.

The famous name – one of the most decorated in the British Army – has now ceased deployment to Afghanistan and await future engagements as and when they arise in the interest of Great Britain.

Dissolution of the Monasteries

Cleeve Abbey and the Lords of Dunster Castle

On 25th June 1198 the medieval Abbey of St Mary at Cleeve was founded. Dedicated to the Blessed Virgin, it was originally named Vallis Florida or Vale of Flowers. Since then the dissolution of the monasteries, destruction of the Abbey Church and subsequent use as a farmhouse have all played a part in the 800-year history of Cleeve Abbey, with a strong association with the Lords of Dunster Castle running throughout.

The early Cistercians at Cleeve were highly successful agriculturalists and also owned one of the four mills at Dunster, a tucking mill and two stocks, all in or near West Street. Here they probably made their own woollen habits of coarse white wool cloth, undyed, unbleached and natural, giving them their name "white monks". In 1346 the Cistercians built the famous 'nunnery' in Dunster, although this was never used by nuns.

The association between Cleeve Abbey and Dunster Castle stretched back to the de Mohuns as the first benefactors. Sir Hugh Luttrell's wife, Catherine Beaumont, used to go regularly on pilgrimage to Cleeve Abbey, as the Dunster Castle accounts show on 11 June 1406: "To my Lady going on pilgrimage to Cleeve, 6d". Twenty years later, in 1430, Sir John Luttrell ordered the Abbot of Cleeve and other freeholders to pay fealty to him or be fined 3d.

By the time of the Dissolution of the Monasteries in the late 1530s there were thirteen monks, an abbot and a prior living at the abbey. A survey in 1533 had found that these monks lived an honest life and were giving a great deal more to charity than other comparable monasteries. However, in 1536 the Act for the Suppression of the Lesser Monasteries stated that all houses with an income of less than £200 were to be closed. Cleeve's income was £155-9s-5¼ d. So in September 1536 the last Abbot, William Dovell, surrendered the abbey. Upon dissolution the Priory buildings and land passed into the hands of the Crown, who then leased the land to John Luttrell, an uncle of Sir John Luttrell (his portrait hangs in the Inner Hall), who had recently inherited the castle.

During the 17th century, Cleeve Abbey became a farm. The cloisters were used as the farmyard with the dormitory probably used as a barn and the rooms below the refectory as stables. A new farmhouse was built shortly afterwards.

In the 1870s the abbey was bought by George Fownes Luttrell. He worked to arrest the decay of the monastic buildings and also carried out the first archaeological excavations of the site. The workmen, supplied by the Luttrells, found the remains of the original church buried under a seven-foot high pile of manure and debris from the original destruction. George stopped all farm work on site and divided the farmhouse into rented cottages.

George Luttrell's work in bringing the railway to Minehead also meant that Cleeve Abbey was within easy reach of tourists for the first time. This was essential for its survival as evinced by Our Lady at Old Cleeve, a nearby place of pilgrimage just to the north-west of Cleeve Abbey, which suffered a decline in pilgrimage and interest after the Reformation; nothing now remains of this site.

The care the Luttrells took over the abbey was noted by author Edward Foord in 1925, who stated that the Abbey and buildings had been "wonderfully well preserved. They are now carefully maintained by the Luttrells, lords of the manor, and furnish an almost unsurpassed example of the domestic portion of a monastery".

In August 1949 the sale of Dunster Castle and its estates meant the Abbey was sold to the Government. In 1984 it passed into the guardianship of English Heritage, under whose care it remains today.

Acknowledgments: Lyte, History of Dunster Part 1. A History of the County of Somerset, vol 2; House of Cistercian Monks – Cleeve Abbey; English Heritage, Teachers' Resource Book; Dunster Church and Priory, Hancock 1905; T. Lambert, History of Dunster; Dissolution of the Monasteries, G W O Woodwar, A Pitkin Guide; Richard Stanton, A Menology of England and Wales, Burns & Oates, Ltd 1892.

Gunpowder, Treason and Plot

Remember, remember the fifth of November
Gunpowder, treason and plot.
We see no reason, why gunpowder treason
Should ever be forgot

The date November 5th celebrates one of the most infamous events in the United Kingdom, one that everyone in Britain has known since childhood and which has embedded itself in our national psyche for hundreds of years; the date of the Gunpowder Plot of 1605.

The conspirators, led by Robert Catesby of Coughton Court (National Trust, Warwickshire), planned to blow up the Houses of Parliament during the State Opening. Their aim was to kill the Protestant King, James I, and to place a Catholic monarch on the throne in his place. One source attributes the plans to Robert Parsons, born in the Quantock village of Nether Stowey, close to Coleridge Cottage.

On the night of November 4 1605, the men placed kegs of gunpowder in the cellars of the Parliament buildings. They planned to ignite it when King James, his eldest son Prince Henry (whose portrait hangs in the Inner Hall) and Queen Ann attended the State Opening the following day. The explosion would have been heard at least five miles away and seen from many miles more, and even if only half the gunpowder had gone off, everyone in the House of Lords and its environs would have been killed instantly. The blast would have been mostly directed upwards, raining debris over a 200-metre radius.

One of the conspirators, Guy Fawkes, was deputed to stay with the gunpowder and ignite it at the opportune moment. However, word of the conspiracy leaked out, and royal officials captured Fawkes with the gunpowder.

The trial of eight of the plotters began on Monday 27 January 1606. Fawkes shared the barge from the Tower to Westminster Hall with seven of his fellow would-be assassins. They were kept in the Star Chamber before being taken to Westminster Hall, where they were displayed on a purpose-built scaffold. The King and his close family, watching in secret, were among the spectators as the Lords Commissioners read out the list of charges.

Fawkes was identified as Guido Fawkes, "otherwise called Guido Johnson". He pleaded not guilty, despite his apparent acceptance of guilt from the moment he was captured.

The outcome was never in doubt. The jury found all of the defendants guilty, and the Lord Chief Justice of England, Sir John Popham of Wellington, Somerset, whose daughter Jane married into the Luttrell family a few years later, proclaimed them guilty of high treason. The Attorney General, Sir Edward Coke, told the court that each of the condemned would be drawn backwards to his death by a horse, his head near the ground. They were to be "put to death halfway between heaven and earth as unworthy of both". Their genitals would be cut off and burnt before their eyes, and their bowels and hearts removed. They would then be decapitated, and the dismembered parts of their bodies displayed so that they might become "prey for the fowls of the air".

On 31 January 1606, Fawkes and three others were dragged from the Tower on wattled hurdles to the Old Palace Yard at Westminster, opposite the building they had attempted to destroy. His fellow plotters were then hanged and quartered. Fawkes was the last to stand on the scaffold. He asked for forgiveness of the King and State, while keeping up his "crosses and idle ceremonies", and aided by the hangman began to climb the ladder to the noose. Then, although weakened by torture, Fawkes managed to jump from the gallows, breaking his neck in the fall and thus avoiding the agony of the latter part of his execution. His lifeless body was nevertheless quartered and, as was the custom, his body parts were then distributed to "the four corners of the kingdom", to be displayed as a warning to other would-be traitors.

News of the attempt on the King's life and trial and execution of the plotters would have reached Dunster by pamphlet; pamphlets were sold on street corners or print shops in London and carried to rural locations immediately. It is tempting and reasonable to think this is how the castle received the news from London, with a footman bringing the pamphlet to George Luttrell in person from the then 'staging post', the Ship Inn (now the Luttrell Arms Hotel).

John Wyndham was High Sheriff of Somerset when the Gunpowder Plot took place, with his cousin, George Luttrell, holding that office four years later in 1609.

The plot provoked strong feelings and the majority of the nation reacted with horror to the sheer indiscriminate killing planned. The foiling of the Gunpowder Plot initiated a wave of national relief at the delivery of the King and his sons, and inspired in the ensuing parliament a mood of loyalty and goodwill, especially from West Somerset, through the work of the Popham and Wyndham families in the interrogation and sentencing of Guy Fawkes and his co-conspirators.

Whilst engaged in this background research I found it of great interest to learn of Dunster Castle's links and associations with the Gunpowder Plot through the Luttrells' marriage to the Popham and Wyndham families, and it came as no surprise to discover that no fewer than seven National Trust properties have direct historic links to the perpetrators.

To this day the Houses of Parliament are still searched by the Yeomen of the Guard just before the State Opening to ensure no latter-day Fawkes is concealed in the cellars, though this is retained as a picturesque custom rather than a serious anti-terrorist precaution (for which, of course, there are proper means).

In celebration of the failed plot King James I ordered that his subjects should have a great bonfire every 5th November, the date the plotters were foiled. The lantern Guy Fawkes carried in 1605 can still be seen in the Ashmolean Museum, Oxford.

With thanks to the archivists, Somerset Heritage Centre, Taunton.

Acknowledgements: The Gunpowder Plot Society; The National Archives, Gunpowder Plot; *The Children's Encyclopaedia of British History*; *The Gunpowder Plot: Parliament & Treason 1605;* People, UK Parliament. *History of Dunster*, Lyte. *Oxford History of Britain 1984*; Kenneth Morgan. Leland's Itinerary, 1542.

Further reading: *Guy Fawkes: The Real Story of the Gunpowder Plot*, Fr Francis Edwards, (1969); *The Gunpowder Plot*, Antonia Fraser, (1996); *English Reformation*, Christopher Haigh (1993); *Investigating the Gunpowder Plot*, Mark Nicholls (1991); Ark to Ashmolean (Gallery 8), Ground Floor, Case Q016.

Acknowledgments and sources

Invasions of England: Battle of Hastings 1066 by Kennedy Hickman

Shaw's Knights of England, vol ii, p12, Lyte P122

Anglo-Saxon Thegn, 449-1066, Mark Harrison 1993

Calendar of Patent Rolls 1461 -1467

Encyclopedia of British History- Children's Revised Edition

Dudley Dodd, NT *Dunster Castle* p44

From Currach to Ketch, The Story of Minehead's Quay Town by John Gilman and Sue Lloyd

National Trust, Dudley Dodd.

Domesday Book, A Complete Translation, Alecto Historical Edition 1992

Anglo-Saxon England, Peter Hunter Blair, 1997

Somerset Victorian County History

The Oxford History of Britain, Oxford University Press 1984

Somerset Historic Environment Record 34164

Dunmonia and the Valley of the Parret, Rev William Greswell 1922

Maxwell Lyte, *Dunster and its Lords* (privately printed) 1066-1881

Encyclopedia of British History 1996

Britannia; Conquest and Resistance 1066-1088

St Thomas of Canterbury, Edwin A Abbot (1898)

The Turbulent Priest (1964) Compton Piers

Medieval Europe, A Short History (1975) Hollister, Warren C.,

The Murder of Thomas a Becket, 1170 Eyewitness to History, www.eyewitnesstohistory.com (1997)

St Thomas Becket biography in Vita S. Thomae, Cantuariensis Archepiscopi et Martyris, ed. in James Robertson, *Materials for the Life of Thomas Becket* (London: Rolls Series, 1875-1885) (7 vols.) Vol. II.

Vita S. Thomae, Cantuariensis Archepiscopi et Martyris, ed. in James Robertson, *Materials for the Life of Thomas Becket*, (London: Rolls Series, 1875-1885) (7 vols.) Vol. II.

Lives Of The Bishops of Winchester - Stephen Hyde Cassan.

The Chronicles of Froissart, John Bourcher [Lord Berners], tr., G C Macaulay, ed. (London : Macmillan, 1908), pp. 99-107]

Monmouth Rebellion, W M Wigfield

A Short History of the English People, J R Green 1874

The Siege and Surrender of Dunster Castle, Emanuel Green, (paperback) published 2011 by British Library, Historical Print Editions

The Portrait of Sir John Luttrell, A Tudor Mystery, String of Pearls Festival Courtauld Gallery, London: 2000

A History of Somerset, Robert Dunning

Men of the 1st Foot Guards at Waterloo and Beyond, Barbara Chambers

Scotch Roll, 15, Edward 111

Dictionary of National Biography, 1885-1900, Volume 63 Wyndham, Thomas (1510?-1553) by Albert Frederick Pollard

With special thanks to the staff of Dunster Castle and volunteers, and to the Archivists, Somerset Heritage Centre, Taunton.

Further Reading

Domesday Book, A Complete Translation, Alecto Historical Edition

Anglo-Saxon England, Peter Hunter Blair 1997

Somerset Victorian County History

The Oxford History of Britain published in 1984

Somerset Historic Environment Record 34164

Dunster and its Lords, 1066-1881, Maxwell Lyte, privately printed

Encyclopaedia of British History 1996

Children's Encyclopaedia of British History 1992

Shaw's Knights of England, vol ii, p12

Chronicles of the White Rose, pp24, 111

Dunster Castle, Dudley Dodd, National Trust, 1999

Taunton Garrison, English Heritage and 'Battle of Sedgemoor', Dudley Dodd.

David Rose 'Battle of Sedgemoor'. Monmouth Rebellion,

Robert War Walks by Richard Holmes

The Reign of Stephen, Kinship, Warfare and Government

What is the Magna Carta?

Heather Whipps Life Sciences June 12, 2012

Battle of Sedgemoor, David Rose

Monmouth Rebellion, Robert Dunning.

Monmouth Rebellion, W M Wigfield

Lives Of The Bishops of Winchester, Stephen Hyde Cassan